Contents

Planning your website

Every successful venture needs a plan, so in this chapter we tackle those sometimes tricky preparation issues that you need to consider before creating your Web pages.

Covers

Chapter One

Introducing the Web

The Internet, or "Net", is a vast collection of interconnected computers spread across the globe providing information on almost any subject imaginable.

To learn more about the coding details of creating Web pages, consider buying "HTML in easy steps".

The World Wide Web (WWW) – more commonly known as the Web – is a "branch" of the Internet and provides access to a vast amount of information through Web pages. In another sense, the Web is really just another way in which millions of people the world over can connect, communicate, learn, and do business.

If you're new to the Internet, see "Internet in easy steps" to better understand how it all works.

Through the Web, a visitor using one computer can access information on another computer which may be close by or a long distance away: in fact, location is almost irrelevant on the Net.

Web pages can contain text, images and other graphics, sound, video and other types of animation and are saved as files stored on thousands of computers across the globe. Related Web pages linked together at the same location make up a website; however, even a single self-contained Web page can be a Web "site".

"Simple" Web pages contain only some text, images and special codes or tags which determine how the elements should appear. These codes that show how Web pages behave are part of a simple computer language known as HyperText Mark-up Language (HTML). More dynamic Web pages can also be created by combining HTML with a scripting language like JavaScript.

To create Web pages, you don't necessarily need to understand HTML as DTP-type software is now available enabling you to concentrate on how you want to design your pages rather than how to actually enter the codes to make them work. Nevertheless, to achieve complex and sometimes tricky-to-set-up special effects, more often than not an in-depth knowledge of HTML can save you time and much "hair-pulling".

Creating a website: an overview

To create your Web pages, here's what you'll need:

- Access to the Internet: for most folks, this means a PC with a cable modem/ADSL or ISDN link provided by an Internet Service Provider (ISP).

- A Web "host" to store and display your website pages.

- Software to create your site. Examples include: Macromedia Dreamweaver, Microsoft FrontPage, Adobe PageMill, NetObjects Fusion, Allaire HomeSite and Adobe GoLive.

Macromedia Dreamweaver MX
Product Overview

The Professional Choice for building websites and Internet applications
The professional choice for building websites and Internet applications Now every member of your development team—designers, developers, and programmers—can work in a single integrated environment to create, build, and manage websites and Internet applications. Macromedia Dreamweaver MX combines its renowned visual layout tools with the rapid web application development features of Dreamweaver UltraDev and the extensive code-editing support of Macromedia HomeSite. So the world's best way to create professional websites is now the easiest way to build powerful Internet applications.

If you need to save money, you can even create HTML Web pages using most basic text editors like Windows Notepad, or a pure text editor like TextPad.

- Web-oriented, graphics design software such as Paint Shop Pro, Adobe Illustrator, Photoshop or ImageReady.

- Knowledge and skills to use the above: this book can help you learn quickly. Persevere. Keep learning. For more complex animations, specialist skills are required.

- Several Web browsers (ideally) installed on your PC to check compatibility – install the most recent versions of Microsoft Internet Explorer and Netscape Navigator. Or website validator software/checking.

- FTP Software to upload your website to your Web host when you're ready to go "live". Web design tools like Dreamweaver include built-in FTP commands. However, examples of separate FTP programs include CuteFTP (www.globalscape.com) and WS_FTP (www.ipswitch.com).

- For business websites: ecommerce online payment processing and optionally database design/adaptation components.

Netiquette and the spirit of the Web

Netiquette is Internet etiquette. Simply having consideration for other online users. Below are two important ways to do just that:

Avoiding spam

No, we're not talking meat. "Spamming" refers to the practice of sending uninvited email and newsclips to vast numbers of users without their permission. This sort of activity is usually frowned upon by many amongst the Internet community. Spamming also helps clog up the Internet for all of us. Two areas where you should not blatantly advertise products or services are amongst newsgroups and mailing lists (see Chapter 15 for more details).

Share something valuable – and gain.

Some of the most effective and eye-catching sites on the Web work well by sharing something of real value. For example: rare, unique, hard-to-find information; an offer of free software; hints and tips on a hot topic; and so on. The Internet and Web have grown popular through the amazing range of information freely available.

Computers can often present a cold, uncaring and indifferent face. You can bring warmth to a Web page by relating your message using content that is familiar to anyone: use images of smiling people; sights, sounds, thoughts, feelings and emotion.

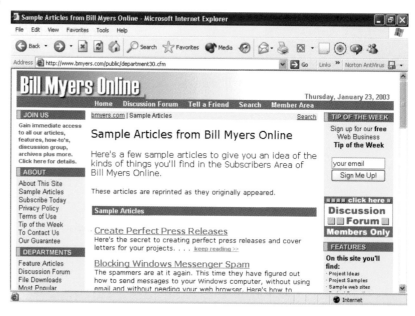

To encourage people to revisit your site, you could provide some free information. The website above (www.bmyers.com) provides an excellent example of this technique. Study this site carefully.

Establishing purpose

Establishing what to include and what to omit from a Web page is a crucial element in the design process. Above all, keep focused on what your website is for. Consider the following guidelines:

- Each Web page has a distinct purpose and central message. Always keep this in mind when designing each page.

- Create a logical hierarchy in how you display information to provide an obvious and easy-to-understand structure.

- Try to make sure a page is neither too "busy" nor contains several prominent elements which fight for attention.

- Balance page components by the subtle use of strong and weak colors, as well as physical size and placement.

For businesses

For businesses, essentially your website is an interactive electronic brochure that helps you sell and market your products and services. Most importantly, your website is also a funnel – a customer "filter" that should be designed to:

- Capture a visitor's email address.

- Make repeated sales.

- Start and maintain a dialog.

Adding fun-type animations, "production" clip art and garish color schemes etc. to a personal website is a matter of taste. However, for a business-oriented website, a much more considered approach is called for (see Chapter 14 for more guidelines).

FREE EBOOK VIDEO
Showing you 100% live examples of what can be created with the all new eBook Generator 3.0

First Name:

Last Name

Email Address:

Download Now

What you decide to include in your Web "brochure" is one aspect. However, what you decide to leave out is probably just as important: resist the urge to include everything about your organization. How: make every word count.

Key point: the good news is, you don't need an expensively designed website to make the site profitable. Arguably, the less "overwhelming" and more considered your website is, the more effective your Web campaign can be. Some of the most profitable websites have a simple structure that doesn't confuse visitors.

Profit tip: consider keeping back half of your website development budget to spend on a careful promotion AND developing a considered search engine submission strategy.

Profiling your target visitor

Before designing your Web pages, learn about your target visitors in detail. Consider:

Getting to know your visitors is crucial to your Web success. Create online forms that engage with visitors and ask key questions. This not only demonstrates that you're interested in what they think but helps you better understand what really motivates your visitors. Correct, reliable and up-to-date focused information has immense value.

- Their approximate age range; the kinds of jobs they perform; are they young or more mature? Younger visitors may prefer a dynamic, highly colorful impact. More mature visitors may react better to something more subtle.

- Where do they live? What language do they speak? Perhaps English is becoming an accepted international language. Yet even English has variations: American, Canadian, International and British. So you may need to consider spelling oddities. Also, be aware that some colors and color combinations have special significance in some cultures. Don't offend; do the research first.

The lower resolution WebTV standard (typically 544 x 378 pixels) that is so popular in North America, may indeed yet grow into a global television standard for displaying Web pages, especially as the Web and television merge ever closer. Watch this standard closely during the next few years. However, many of today's Web pages cannot be viewed properly using WebTV.

- Decide on a minimum PC specification. Do you want to design for slower PCs (say 486 processors) or faster ones?

- Establish which operating systems they're using. Microsoft Windows, Apple Mac, even Linux might be relevant.

- If you intend to use sound or multimedia, be sure that your visitors have PCs that can process your sound and video files reliably, and how they may react if they meet problems.

- Most users now use at least 800 x 600 (SuperVGA) resolution. Nevertheless, still check (see the HOT TIP). Know your target visitors and your answers will become clear.

By asking sometimes difficult questions early on in the design process, you can design correctly first time, and decide the level of sophistication you can safely use without alienating visitors.

Creating a design strategy

To create Web pages that get results, essentially you need to complete two main tasks:

- Build HTML Web code that meets the current standards.

- Devise designs that display quickly, are interesting, engaging, attractive and "tuned" to the interests of your target visitors.

Sounds easy, doesn't it? Let's take a closer look.

You can gain ideas about how to design your Web pages by seeing how other, similar websites appear. Note carefully what you like and dislike, then adjust your designs to create even better standards.

Arguably, one of the key reasons why so many commercial websites are failing is that they have a cold corporate look and feel. Many of those who are succeeding, however, get personal with prospects and customers alike. In these "lucky" websites, people are treated as individuals; warmly and with respect. So why not use these simple insights to build your Web success too?

Use offscreen planning to get started

Before setting to work with your Web page design software, switch off your PC, get pen and paper and note down your initial ideas: what you want to achieve from your website. Brainstorm with colleagues or friends if possible to "magnify" your ideas.

Create an outline "tree" structure placing your Home/Index page at the top. Then create the main "link" pages that feed down from your Home or Index page.

Draft out the opening Web page in more detail. Aim to create a logical opening structure and try out different approaches. Keep it appropriate to your visitors; make it inviting but simple to navigate.

Fourteen key Web guidelines to help you succeed

However you eventually decide to create your pages, some things are essential to know before you get down to work. Consider the following guidelines to help you really get started well:

If your Web pages are dealing with particularly complex topics, provide information in "bite-sized" chunks. Use (active) space to provide plenty of "breathing space". Also, consider using short paragraphs of less than 3–5 lines. Why? Reading onscreen demands more from the eye: simplify to get better results.

1   For those in business, a true domain Web page address is *essential* these days for all sorts of reasons (see Chapter 14 for detailed guidelines). If you skimp in business, it shows.

2   The fast pace of modern living for many means that available time can be in short supply: help your visitors by making sure your pages load quickly (more about this hugely important point later).

3   First impressions on the Web really do count. Aim to create a great impression on the first visit. Within the first 60 seconds of logging onto your Home/Index page, a visitor forms an opinion (sometimes subconsciously) about your site, and therefore about you, your company, or the organization that you represent.

4   When considering what to include in a Web page, usually many choices emerge. Try to put yourself in the place of a visitor and ask yourself what they would really want to see. Make a short list, then leave out anything else not essential. Sometimes, less really is more.

If you use familiar components (like the same toolbars, fonts and tables) and follow the same information delivery plan across your pages, visitors know what to expect. This more considered approach helps them engage with your site and absorb information more easily (and, most importantly, act on it).

5   Don't provide too many choices – this only overwhelms and confuses people. Limit page/site navigation options to between 7–10 maximum. These could be buttons, icons, individual parts of a larger image, or simply text components.

6   Aim to make your Web pages attractive, compelling and engaging. This book can help show how. Create a consistent design style that does not overpower the central message.

7   Carefully focus design aspects towards your target audience to ensure they can quickly identify with what you're saying or offering.

8   If your website essentially provides information, use fast-loading graphics that support your text. Unless you have a

special reason, consider carefully whether to use special animation effects like Shockwave, Flash and Java elements.

Another potentially useful way to develop ideas for your website is to brainstorm with friends or colleagues. Each can write down initial thoughts – however wacky – then collectively discuss ideas. Finally, build a master plan from the results.

9   If your website is primarily aimed at entertaining or advertising, Shockwave and Java-type animations may help enhance your presentation. However, always consider your visitors – and provide options. Define the kind of computer equipment they're using, then modify your designs to match.

10   Remember, generally visitors don't like having to scroll down a page in order to read it. However, compelling sales-oriented material may be tolerated providing it's not too long (say, over 4 screen-lengths). Make a judgement here.

11   Don't force visitors to have to scroll from left to right to read your text. Use narrow newspaper-like columns.

12   Generally, visitors are not keen to read what they consider to be unnecessary material. One way around this problem is to briefly include the essential information first. Then next to this, insert links to other pages that contain the details.

Fast-loading rollover links in the form of simple graphical buttons can provide quick and easy access to all the essential pages in your website. Good quality Web design software often includes predesigned buttons ready for you to use.

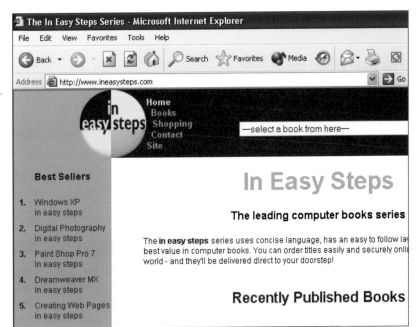

13   For businesses, design your entire Web operation to compel visitors to voluntarily leave their email address with you. Targeted email addresses are like liquid gold, the offline equivalent of your mailing list. If you don't capture a visitor's address on the first visit, you may never have another chance to sell them something. Use ezines, quizzes, competitions, draws etc. to continually provide "magnetic" variety.

Making your website easy to use should be a high priority. This doesn't mean that your Web presentation has to be boring. Effective communication can be achieved through providing relevant and valuable information with carefully considered color combinations.

14   Never forget the three most important reasons why visitors are "turned off" by a website:

–   When what they see is boring, or suggests hype or lies.

–   When pages take too long to display.

–   When the site is confusing to use.

Meeting the HTML standard

The HyperText Markup Language (HTML) is still the main standard that is used to create working Web pages. HTML is continually being developed, improved and updated. You need to ensure that your pages meet the current HTML standard, and to decide how far back you want to go to support earlier Web browsers. See your Web design software manuals for details.

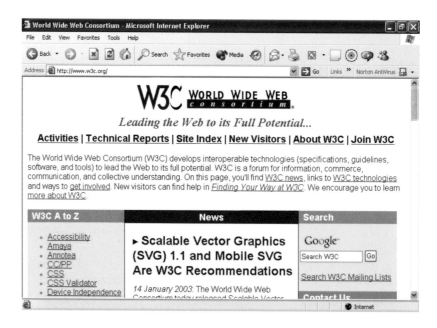

Establishing when to stop

No one should presume to tell you when your Web page design is "right"; only you as the designer really know that. But you can reach a stage beyond which any further contribution you make doesn't improve the result. So how can you decide when to stop?

Lessons from the artists

How often, as children, have many of us created a drawing or painting of which we're proud, only to become so excited that we tried to "make it a little better"? By the time we realized the mistake, it was too late – the picture was spoiled. And as grown-ups, many professional artists providing drawing and painting workshops press home the point to their students: "Don't overdo it", "Know when to stop". Some even say: "When you think the drawing is *almost* complete, it *is* complete and that's the time to stop."

Sometimes the desire to create something special can lead to adding complex cutting-edge features to a Web page. This may be fine but, if ill-considered, can result in a "one-browser-only" Web page – not so good for businesses. Test drive your designs with several browsers and get second opinions before going live.

As a Web page is essentially a graphical medium, this kind of advice can be relevant here too. As we design our pages, it's easy to become so absorbed in the process and to so enjoy it that we can sometimes lose sight of the overall goal: to create an attractive, usable and interesting offering that people will want to revisit.

Harnessing the power of active space

Space has power. Yes, even empty areas of a Web page can deliver a powerful message in their own right. Considered use of empty space is not really empty at all: it's active. This "active space" adds to the overall offering. So many Web pages now are filled with pointless, confusing "clutter" that those which are designed with economy in mind can stand out.

In conventional publishing, the power of active white space has long been accepted. In the daily newspapers, periodically we see advertisements which take up an entire page, but which might perhaps contain a single entity or small amount of carefully considered text. Yet our eyes, which arguably are not trained to expect this in a newspaper, are drawn to the page so that such advertisements can be very effective in gaining our attention.

We can also use this method in our Web designs with just as much success. Most people still essentially use the Web to discover information or buy something, or both. In this way, we can use white space to frame what we want the visitor to focus on.

Choosing your Web host

A Web host stores your pages and makes them available to visitors. Literally thousands of companies worldwide are available that you can employ to host your website. What's more, the Web host you choose need not even be located in your own country. So how do you go about choosing the one that's right for you? Consider the following "ideal" guidelines:

A good way to really check out the claims a Web host makes is to speak to some of their customers one-to-one.

- Technical support: 7-day, 24-hour email/live support with reply in under 12 or 24 hours – under 4 hours is better.

- Web space: 100 Mb will almost certainly provide enough space for about 1000 pages. In practice, 20 Mb may be more than enough for most people, unless you're storing large-capacity files available for download.

- Contract duration: ideally, get a "no minimum contract" deal so you can cancel at any time. Some offer discounts if you pay 1 year in advance.

- Unlimited hits: a "hit" is when a visitor views your page.

- Mirroring and peering: peering and mirroring ensure your site will always provide the fastest connection speeds.

- Email addresses: ideally get unlimited (or enough) email addresses so that you can create variations e.g.: orders@ yourcompany.com and support@yourcompany.com.

Visit some sites hosted by a Web host to evaluate their claims. Check things like speed of access and how long Web pages they host take to load, and so on.

- Autoresponders: unlimited (see Chapter 14). Essential for business websites.

- "Downtime": during downtime, your website is not visible (Example: Web hosts need to perform their own maintenance to keep things running smoothly). A good host will have 99.5%+ "uptime" leaving 0.5% for downtime.

- Cost: the less you need to pay, the better. However, remember: you generally get what you pay for. For business sites especially, Web host reliability should take first priority.

- CGI bin: providing special scripts, forms, etc.

- E-commerce capability/support: vital for business sites.

Web page design basics

In this chapter, we learn about the basic rules and components that affect most Web pages and tackle some key issues to help you avoid possible pitfalls later on.

Covers

Chapter Two

Popular Web design tools

Often, the most attractive and appealing Web pages have benefited from the skills of professional Web page designers and graphic artists. These skills certainly cost money, but the results can set your site apart from the crowd.

"How can I create Web pages?" A fair question. Let's tackle it. If you're feeling really brave, you can create HTML using any text editor like TextPad or Windows Notepad. However, for most folks, those tools are ideal for fine-tuning but not much help in getting your creative juices to flow. The best Web design tools now take a graphical or DTP-like approach to creating websites. Popular programs include:

- Adobe PageMill and its much more powerful multimedia-oriented big brother, GoLive! (www.adobe.com/products/golive/main.html).

- Dreamweaver from Macromedia (www.macromedia.com/software/dreamweaver/).

- FrontPage from Microsoft (www.microsoft.com/frontpage/).

- Fusion from NetObjects (www.websitepros.com).

- HotMetal Pro from SoftQuad (www.hotmetalpro.com).

- Aracnophilia from Paul Lutus (www.arachnoid.com). At the time of writing, Aracnophilia was described as free careware.

Popular Web graphics tools

Most special effects that you might want to create in Web pages can be achieved using the superb Paint Shop Pro (www.jasc.com). Or you can choose excellent tools from Adobe's range: Illustrator, Photoshop and ImageReady. Other powerful graphics tools with a strong following include Fireworks from Macromedia and CorelDRAW!

Creating animations and multimedia

Wizards can do the bulk of Web page creation for you. Simply answer some basic questions and the software does the rest. You can then make final adjustments manually. Microsoft FrontPage and Publisher are two great wizard-driven applications.

You can create simple animated GIF sequences (Chapter 10) using tools like GIF Animator (www.mindworkshop.com/alchemy/alchemy.html) or Adobe After Effects. To create high quality, fast-loading Flash animations, look at Flash from Macromedia (www.macromedia.com/). These are all powerful applications and so take time to learn. Once they're familiar, quality and productivity can soar providing excellent value for money.

Three types of Web page

Any website can be made up of three types of Web pages:

- The Home page: often the first page which a visitor sees (sometimes a Welcome page precedes this).

In the NetObjects Fusion website structure map below, you can see the various levels that make up the site hierarchy:

Throughout this book, we have included some JavaScript examples. If you use these, make sure you type every single character correctly, and, where you see quotes, use straight quotes like this ("), not curly quotes like this ("). Ideally, spend some time learning the basics of JavaScript first.

Home/Index page

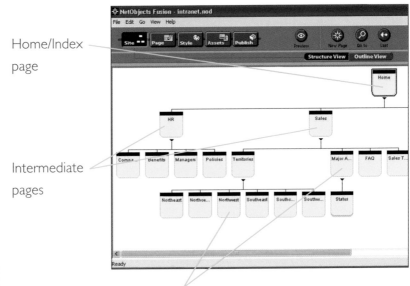

Intermediate pages

Content pages can have several levels. Ideally, ensure that a visitor can easily move to any page within about 3 mouse clicks

A new breed of website has now developed. These "direct response", aggressive marketing-oriented mini-sites usually have few links. They may have 4 or fewer pages, to limit the choices open to the visitor so as to get the single, most wanted response (e.g. an order, an email address or signing up an affiliate) very quickly.

In these sites, the visitor stays, acts or simply goes. Many of them appear to be highly successful commercially.

- Intermediate pages: these are the pages which are "the next level down", immediately accessible from the Home/Index page. Usually, you'll want to place a link back to the Home/Index page from each of these intermediate pages.

- Content pages: these contain topic details and are usually accessible from Intermediate pages. Often, Content pages may also include a link back to the Home page in addition to other relevant links.

The value of first impressions

Someone once said: "You never get a second chance to make a good first impression", and on the Web this has never been more true. Here, looks and usability are everything! When someone accesses your website for the first time, they don't know you – or trust you, and many people are naturally suspicious – especially in view of all the over-hyped stories that circulate in the media from time to time about the Internet.

People appreciate being considered. "Be professional" – a simple statement that can have big implications in your Web design (and sales, if you're in business). Good design doesn't have to be overly ornate or flashy. Simple, clear navigation, some carefully selected quality images and useful, valuable information have their own message, which visitors can pick up quickly. Just build trust.

There's a great tendency now on many websites to include as much action, animation, electronic tricks, flashing logos, graphics or icons as possible. Resist this urge and instead let the three C's dictate your overall design:

Once you've stimulated visitors to visit your Web pages regularly, to maintain interest remember to update your pages regularly and let visitors know when you'll be doing this to help create a sense of expectation.

- **Consistency:** try to create a similar style of presentation across all the pages in your site. Visitors then know what to expect and this helps them absorb information more easily.

- **Color:** contrast helps an item stand out or blend in.

- **Content:** within the first few seconds of seeing your Home/Index page, your visitors should know the main benefits of what you're providing.

Minimizing Home/Index page download time

Every second counts on the Net. You can save precious seconds by applying the design techniques you'll learn in this book. You may have superb content but if something results in your visitor not waiting until it has downloaded, all your efforts are wasted.

Even though more and more visitors may nowadays be getting faster Broadband Internet connections, if you design for slower modems (28.8Kbps), then your pages serve the maximum number of users properly.

Key point: ensure your Home page downloads within about 25–30 seconds using a 28.8 Kbps modem – ideally within 10 seconds. Results of recent studies suggest we're getting more impatient and may move on to another website if we don't get sufficient visual payback within 10 seconds of the page starting to load!

Utilizing the power of headlines

One of the best ways to let visitors know what you're offering quickly is with carefully worded headlines placed at the top of your pages, at every vertical screen height, and at other key locations.

Words provide the "glue" that holds your Web presentation together.
Nevertheless, the Web is essentially a graphical medium. So endeavor to make your Web pages colorful, engaging, vibrant and lively.

1 Your main aim is to catch the attention of your visitor with a powerful "what's-in-it-for-me?" question immediately answered through your headline.

2 The most important benefit of your website/page should be made absolutely clear in the main Home/Index page headline. This is where you'll keep or lose a new visitor.

3 The other main benefits of your website, product or service can then be listed logically in your remaining headlines.

On your Home/Index page, ask your visitor to bookmark your site. Also, ask them again on several other pages, just in case they forget.

If you're successful, your visitor will probably be motivated enough to continue exploring your website and indeed, that is the main reason for highlighting your headlines. Congratulations!

Always put strong benefits first!

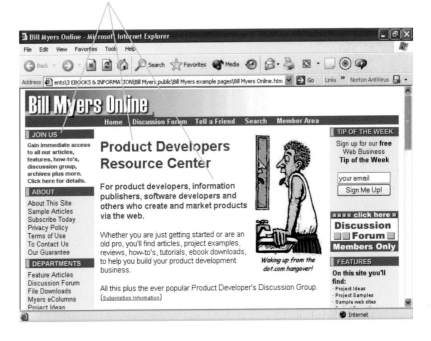

Tables: the cornerstone of design

All browsers support tables. A HTML table is, in its simplest form, a grid of cells laid out in rows/columns. Each cell can contain text, numerical data, an image or even another table (a "nested" table). Presenting information using tables is one of the simplest yet most powerful techniques available to Web designers. For example:

- Correct use of HTML tables ensures neatness and order are demonstrated over a range of Web browsers.

- Information can be presented in precise row and column format. Newsletter-type presentations are then possible.

Tables help align information and objects neatly. You can even make table borders invisible

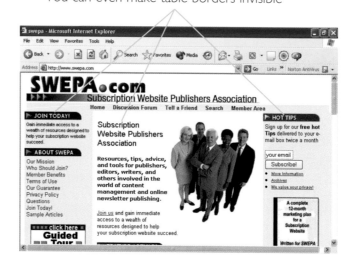

- A variety of attributes can be applied to tables/cells including: different shades, applying/hiding borders, changing cell size, spacing and padding (the empty space around a cell).

- Tables provide the illusion that text, numbers and images can be positioned independently anywhere on a Web page.

You can change the look of a table by combining adjacent cells (spanning) and through inserting a table into the desired cell of another table. Usually, the table background takes precedence over the Web page background. However, if no background color is specified, the properties of the Web page usually apply.

Newspaper-type columns make for easier reading.

Sometimes you may not even need to use tables. Simple, unobtrusive horizontal lines can help separate categories and information to provide a greater sense of order.

To ensure empty table cells display properly in Netscape browsers, insert " " (without the quotes) inside the <TD> tags in your HTML code.

2 Color, contrast and quality graphics bind the theme together.

Creating fixed or variable sized tables

Your Web design software should allow you to specify the size of a table either in pixels or percentages (at least). Therefore, choose:

- Pixels to create a table size that stays the same irrespective of the browser used. Benefit: you know that a table will display the same on different browsers. Drawback: if a browser window is too small, a visitor may have to scroll horizontally to view all the information (bad Web design trait).

- Percentages when you want a visitor's browser to resize the table on-the-fly to match the current size of a visitor's browser window. Main drawback: as you lose control of the design, you may not know for sure how a table will appear.

Using HTML HEIGHT and WIDTH tags in your tables

Normally, Netscape browsers may not display any information within a table until all the graphics have been downloaded into the browser (in later versions, this trait may change).

However, by specifying values in the HEIGHT and WIDTH tags in HTML, you can ensure your visitors can immediately read the text in your tables while the remaining information is downloading.

How WIDTH and HEIGHT tags are shown in HTML

If you want to display information in a precisely defined layout – like a poem, for example – occasional use of the <PRE> tag in HTML provides the simplest solution. Remember, <PRE> preserves the exact character and line spacing/break sequences. <PRE> is also useful for creating perfectly aligned columns of text. See "HTML in easy steps" for more information.

```
<BODY BGCOLOR=#FFFFFF onLoad="MM_preloadImages('images/s122-c86-14-17b4_0
<TABLE WIDTH=752 BORDER=0 CELLPADDING=0 CELLSPACING=0>
  <TR>
    <TD valign="top" width="288" rowspan="2">
      <table width="100%" border="0" cellpadding="0" cellspacing="0" heig
        <tr>
          <td width="288" height="2479" valign="top">
            <p><a href="members/becoming-a-member.html"><img src="images/
" height="31" alt="Members section"></a><a href="questions/faq.html" onMo
ame="Image14" border="0" src="images/s122-c86-14-17b4_11-over.gif" width=
            <table width="90%" border="0" cellspacing="0" cellpadding="0"
              <tr>
                <td class="body" valign="top"> <iframe height="300" width
                  <p><a href="questions/press-release1.html"><b><font col
```

Using a quick loading header table to keep visitors entertained

If you insert most of the main content of a Web page within a table, sometimes a situation can develop in which the page background loads first, followed (perhaps minutes later) by the text and graphics.

Sometimes, you may not want to force your visitor to wait until the full page table has loaded. To avoid this situation, you could create a separate, quick-loading table which contains key information that relates to what the page is about and place this at the top of your Web page.

This smaller table will then display before the main table and your visitors have something to view while the main table is downloading. This simple technique can also be usefully employed where you are including slower loading components, like a multimedia Flash sequence or larger sized graphics.

Presenting information using lists

Listed information can be displayed in HTML Unordered or Ordered list format. Let's examine the differences:

The unordered list defined

An unordered list does not have a numbered sequence. Usually, bullets are used to highlight each entry. Example uses include:

- Displaying text without a numbered or logical sequence.

- Showing a nonspecific sequence of events.

- Displaying entries indented/nested within the previous item.

In HTML, to create an unordered type list, use the <UL> and </UL> tags. To create an ordered list, use the <OL> and </OL> tags.

To choose disc, circle or square bullets, add the word "type" after the List HTML tag <LI>. Then choose disc, circle or square e.g.:

```
<UL>
    <LI TYPE=SQUARE> Line 1 with a square bullet
</UL>
```

When entered properly in HTML, this would display as:

■ Line 1 with a square bullet

To display a list of terms and their meanings on a Web page, you can use the following Definition-type list HTML tags: <DL>, </DL>, <DT>, and <DD>.

What is an ordered list?

An ordered list uses a numbered sequence, ideal for:

- Displaying a logical structure, sequence or flow. (In the example below, in the top section, you can see the HTML code and, in the bottom section, how the sequence displays.)

- Indenting list entries as for unordered list entries.

Although other list commands may be available, some browsers may interpret these commands differently. Usually, only the ordered and unordered list commands behave in the most consistent way in most browsers.

```
If you are interested in our offer and you would like to get your free copy of
you will need to :|
<ol>
    <li>agree to the AVG Free Edition license agreement
    <li>fill in the simple questionaire form
    <li>download the program distribution package
    <li>check your email - you will get your private AVG serial number via email.
    <li>install the program
</ol>
```

If you are interested in our offer and you would like to get your free copy of AVG 6.0 Anti-Virus System, you will need to :

1. agree to the AVG Free Edition license agreement
2. fill in the simple questionaire form
3. download the program distribution package
4. check your email - you will get your private AVG serial number via email.
5. install the program

Establishing ideal page width

In Web page design, the target design space is the visitor's browser window. To decide the desired width (and height) of your Web pages, the topic of resolution comes into play.

Picture resolution defined

The resolution of a display monitor is the total number of pixels used to display the picture. A pixel is a single dot of light on a display monitor. The more pixels used, the better the resolution and therefore the quality of the picture. Current popular screen resolutions in pixels include:

If you decide to use percentages instead of pixels as your Web page width parameter, your pages can be set to occupy 100% of the browser window, and so won't leave any wasted or blank empty space. The drawback is, you lose full control of the design.

- 640 x 480 – now the older VGA standard (that is, 640 pixels wide by 480 pixels high = 307,200 pixels).

- 800 x 600 – the popular SuperVGA standard (480,000 pixels).

- 1024 x 768 pixels – an ideal size for 19" monitors or greater (786,432 pixels).

Several different browsers and display monitor resolutions are currently available and you – as the designer – don't know which combination a visitor may be using.

Deciding on your page width

If you design your Web pages for say 800 x 600 or larger, and a visitor is viewing in 640 x 480, their browser automatically provides a horizontal scrollbar at the bottom of their browser window. To view all information on your pages, they will probably have to keep scrolling back and forth horizontally.

Nevertheless, try to ensure that your visitors will not have to view your site with a horizontal scrollbar. Your visitor may decide that this is simply not worth the hassle and leave.

Many PC users don't maximize their browser window to full screen width, in order to have quick access to other open windows. Therefore, even 700 pixels width may not be available.

Thankfully, most users are now viewing in at least 800 x 600, and some space is taken up with the scrollbars so you won't have the full 800 pixels to use. Consider the guide below:

- 640 x 480 provides about 600 pixels of useful width.

- 800 x 600 provides about 780 pixels of useable width.

- 1280 x 1084 provides about 1200 pixels of useable width.

Establishing ideal page length

A key goal is to ensure the content of each entire Web page fits within the physical space of one screen, so visitors don't have to scroll down to find the information they want.

However, this is not always possible or preferable especially for business-oriented pages: a longer sales message can be more successful if you don't break off at a crucial moment! Consider the following general guidelines:

1 Keep your page lengths as short as possible. Try to fit all of the current topic into fewer than 1 or 2 screens.

2 Provide clear links to the next page in the sequence and to other related pages.

3 If you can't meet the condition is Step 1, ensure you don't force your visitors to scroll down more than 4 screen-heights as an absolute maximum.

4 To minimize the number of times a visitor has to click on the scroll buttons, and to make navigation to key parts easier, consider using index/bookmark pointers at the top or start of the Web page. An index pointer is simply any text or graphic link which, when clicked, takes the visitor to the corresponding part of the page.

5 At the bottom of each page, consider placing a link back to the index at the top of the page and links to other pages in the sequence.

 Provide links to all the main pages in your website on every page and try to make sure that a visitor can get to any page in your site within 3 mouse clicks. Providing a Sitemap or Table of Contents page can help meet this goal.

For personal websites, micro-businesses that provide one or two products or services, and some small predominantly information-providing websites, sometimes your strategy can make more sense by putting everything on one carefully designed scrollable page. Only you can really decide here. If unsure, you can always test different versions and ask visitors for their reactions. Ideally, observe the 4-screen-height limit to avoid irritating visitors.

Hyperlinks, buttons, icons, toolbars

A hyperlink is a link to another part of the same Web page, a separate Web page, or to another Web page or location on the Internet. Hyperlinks can be made using text or a graphic object. Hyperlinks are discussed in more depth in Chapter 5. Popular graphic links use buttons and icons and may be arranged in horizontal rows or vertical columns to form navigation toolbars.

Some of the best websites follow a simple design theme, with technologically exotic components deliberately kept to a minimum. In a highly cluttered Web, the central theme of most sites still revolves around the sharing of information. Open space and simplicity often stand out and make the task of discovering and learning easier.

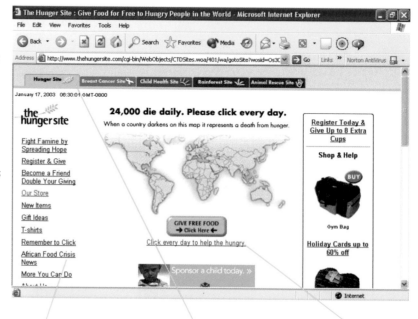

Current-page navigation   "Top-level" site-wide navigation   Additional or highlighted navigation options

As buttons are essentially small graphics, avoid including too much detail within a button. Also, make the purpose of each button instantly recognizable.

The power of a toolbar

Examples of good websites display a thoughtful layout and include navigation aids on *every* page – not just on the Home/Index page. A popular way of providing this feature is to use a toolbar offering a clear at-a-glance outline of the entire website structure.

To make the job of Web page design easier, you can buy Web page components like buttons, icons, backgrounds, and clip art especially prepared for use in Web pages. For examples, see: www.webspice.com/.

Traditional contact information

Surprisingly, many websites still don't include traditional contact information, like mailing address, phone and fax numbers. Web users are naturally suspicious of any new medium like the Internet, and not including basic familiar contact information does not help ease that feeling in many.

1 Appreciate that it is essential to provide clear and correct basic contact information if you want people to contact you. Some people may prefer to use phone or fax instead of email.

2 Include as many different contact methods as possible in your website – ideally: mail address (company name), contact person, phone, fax, and email.

To have your email pre-sorted and sent to one address, you can use email address variations. For example: we know that all emails sent to "orders@yourdomain.com" are sales, while those sent to "feedback@yourdomain.com" relate to feedback messages. Those who send to "help@yourdomain.com" want assistance, and so on.

3 Consider including contact details on all pages that make up your site to ensure that visitors always have immediate and easy access to contact you for more information or order goods or services.

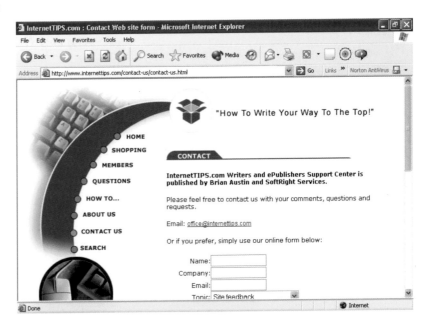

Advert banners and buttons

On the Web, page banners are everywhere. Essentially, they're the Web equivalent of TV advertisements. Banners can be animated or static, small like buttons, or take up most of the page width. You can create a banner advert as an animated GIF image (Chapter 7) or by inserting some HTML code where you want it to appear.

If you want to use high-quality photos in a banner, you can convert the images to JPEG format and use simple JavaScript to create an animated banner.

Attractive invitation   Good color contrast   Clear call to action

Guidelines:

1   Banners usually slow down the loading of a Web page.

2   To avoid creating too many conflicting elements or making a page too "busy", avoid placing banners larger than 468 × 60 (pixels) and limit the quantity to a maximum of 2 per page.

Banner exchange banners placed at the top of a page can be indexed by a search engine before the engine finds your own page information. This will almost certainly cause it to reduce your ranking. Remedy: don't put banners on the Home/ Index page and, if you do use them, site banners at the bottom of pages.

3   Usually, it's best to avoid placing advertisement banners at the top of a page: a new visitor is being prompted to click on the banner and possibly move away from your site – even before reading the current page. Instead, if you're going to use banners, why not place them at the bottom of a page?

4   To properly assess the success of a banner, you need to measure the "Clickthrough" and "Conversion" rates over an extended period of time. Clickthrough rates how many clicks a banner receives. Conversion measures how many people bought as a result of clicking a specified banner.

5   Try to ensure a banner color scheme does not clash with your page colors and make sure there's adequate color contrast between the two.

Installing an email link on a page

Email is one of the easiest ways for your visitors to contact you. Arguably, most visitors already have a default email program installed and set up on their PC. Consider other advantages:

- Sending an email costs much less than sending an equivalent mail letter.

- An email can be received in seconds.

- Time zone and physical location differences become irrelevant. We can collect email when it's convenient to us.

- We don't have to be present to receive email.

To include an email link on a Web page, perform the following:

Here's how email works. Each recipient "rents" a storage area called an email box on a powerful PC connected to the Internet called a mail server. An authorized user can then periodically examine his or her email box and download any messages as desired.

1   You can easily include an email link on your Home page and optionally every other page in your website. Usually, this is a simple operation using DTP-like Web design software. The resulting HTML looks something like this:

```
<A HREF="mailto:brian@yourcompany.com">Send Mail</A>
```

2   Here, we've gone one step further. In the example below, when a visitor clicks on the "Send Mail" link, their email program should open a new email window addressed to brian@yourcompany.com with "Mail Me" pre-entered into the Subject field (key point: notice the exact placement of the question mark in the following example):

```
<A HREF="mailto:brian@yourcompany.com?Subject=Mail Me">Send Mail</A>
```

A visitor can then quickly and easily enter their email message and click their Send button. Note: for the MAILTO command above to work, your relevant Web pages must first be published to your Web space. Also, your email "link" can be made up using plain text, a button or any other graphical component.

Introducing DHTML and CSS

Dynamic HTML or DHTML is essentially a more recent enhancement of plain HTML. DHTML is HTML that is made more dynamic by enabling it to work with scripting components, such as JavaScript (Chapter 10). As you might expect, DHTML is much more powerful than HTML and can help make your Web pages more animated and interactive. For example, with DHTML, a company logo or opening navigation components can be merged in from various directions to quickly form the complete logo or navigation block in a central area of the page. Or text/graphics can be made to fly in or off the screen in various ways.

If you include DHTML components in your Web pages, visitors using earlier browsers may not be able to view them, or such pages may look "wrong". However, statistics show that most users now surf the Net using v4 (or later) browsers which are fine for viewing DHTML components.

Elsewhere this book has stated that it's important to include a textual description for each graphic used. You could also consider providing a text-only version of your website, or perhaps including equivalent text descriptions of all graphics used, towards the base of your pages.

When the page loads, the main navigation bar starts to appear...

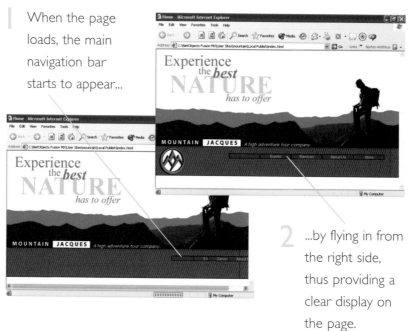

2 ...by flying in from the right side, thus providing a clear display on the page.

Channel Definition Format = Push technology

Channel Definition Format (CDF) (Active Channels) – another development. With the usual HTML-based pages, a Web designer creates a "channel" and CDF document. Visitors can freely "subscribe" to a specific channel and receive regular bulletins. Updates can be downloaded to a visitor's hard drive for offline viewing when convenient. No longer the popular choice.

Cascading Style Sheets (CSS)

CSS is an extension of HTML. A Cascading Style Sheet provides you with a way to control many Web page text- and spacing-related parameters at the same time and so save a lot of re-editing time on larger websites. CSS comes in three main varieties: embedded, linked and inline:

It's easy to get carried away with DHTML special effects. However, these usually work best when applied carefully so as not to overwhelm a Web page, or risk taking your visitors' attention away from the main message of your page. Think through your DHTML strategy carefully first.

- **Embedded CSS**: here a block of CSS is inserted at the start of a page to control how the page is displayed.

- **Linked CSS**: uses a .css document and other HTML pages are then linked to it. The .css document controls the look of those pages to which it is linked. By editing the .css document, you can change the look of all the pages that are linked to it at the same time. With hundreds or even thousands of pages linked to a .css page, just imagine how considered use of this approach at the planning stage of an ambitious Web design can save huge amounts of time and effort later.

- **Inline CSS**: provides a way to change a single HTML tag and so allows you to fine-tune your designs.

In raw HTML, you may often see these symbols: <!-- and --> with some HTML or text inserted inside. These are "comment" symbols and hide the style sheet from older browsers that cannot understand Cascading Style Sheets (CSS).

Below is an example of embedded CSS. This is placed between the <HEAD> and </HEAD> tags in a HTML document:

```
<STYLE>
<!—
BODY {font-family: Times New Roman, Serif; color: black;}
H1 {font-family: Verdana, Arial, Helvetica; font-size: 150%; color: green;}
H2 {font-family: Verdana, Arial, Helvetica; font-size: 120%; color: green;}
TABLE {border: opx solid black; padding: 4px;}
TD.head {background-color: #808080;}
.verdana{font-family: Arial, Sans-serif;}
—>
</STYLE>
```

You can discover much more about CSS at the W3C website. Go to: http://www.w3. org/Style/css/.

CSS is supported in the following browsers and all later versions: Microsoft Internet Explorer v3 and Netscape Navigator v4.

Installing a hit counter

A hit counter records the number of times a page is visited. If you use a conventional hit counter, its position is determined by the HTML code, so you place this type of hit counter as you would any other graphic element. However, a counter makes a page load a little slower.

In a multi-page website, it's also possible to have several counters on different pages, but each would need a different reference in your HTML code.

The counter design can be simple or ornate and through varying the design in relation to the rest of your Web page, you can make a counter stand out, or ensure it takes a minor role by blending it in with the page content.

Deciding whether to include a hit counter

Sometimes, displaying a hit counter can be more trouble than it's worth. Consider:

- If your pages do not receive a lot of visitors, you're advertising this fact to everyone. For a personal website, this may not be an issue. However, for a business-oriented site, low hit counts, perhaps unfairly, suggest a below-par business.

- Alternatively, if you have a high number of hits to your site, visitors may doubt your claims and perhaps not believe the figures are genuine and therefore assume that you have artificially inflated the figures, which may then lead them to doubt any other claims you may make on your site.

Installing a Web page counter

If you decide to include a hit counter, talk to your Internet Service Provider. Some will install a counter for you. Although you can include the HTML code for your counter, since a counter integrates with your Internet Service Provider's Web servers, they may also need to carry out some setup work. Liaise closely.

Ideally, opt for software such as WebTrends (www.netiq.com/webtrends/default.asp) or WebLog that track the number of hits discreetly so that only you have access to the true figures (plus other key information like visitor locations, browser types used).

Avoiding dead URL links

A dead URL link is a link to a Web address that no longer exists or to a page that has been moved to another location. Daily, thousands of Web pages are being modified, updated, moved, reopened and closed. If you include links to other Web addresses in Web pages, before publishing your pages to the Web, make sure all such links are still correct. You can then make any changes necessary before publishing or updating your Web pages.

Once your website is active, regularly check the validity of your Web links, to avoid irritating your visitors with a "The page cannot be displayed" message, as shown below:

There are few events that annoy visitors more than being asked to click on a link that subsequently leads nowhere. Make sure all your URLs are up-to-date and valid.

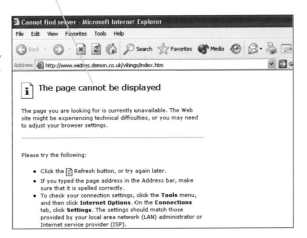

Smart organizations go much further by providing active assistance and making helpful suggestions if a page address a visitor enters is no longer valid.

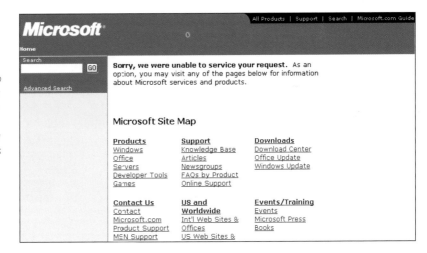

Updating your pages regularly

Once a visitor has viewed your website – and likes what they see – one of the best ways to keep your visitor coming back again and again is to update your site with new fresh content regularly – and make sure that people know that you're updating your pages. If you have carefully provided what your visitors want, updated information that is valuable to them gives them a firm reason to revisit your website, providing further options to build trust.

You can use a "What's New" section as the focus point for your updates. You can also let previous visitors know when your site has received important updates: simply send them an email, but get their permission to do this first, ideally using an option or check box on one of your online forms, or simply send an email and ask.

While looking for fresh content to keep your pages up-to-date, try to think up new ways in which you can further your aims. For example, in the example on the immediate right, a Virus Alert page tells users about the latest threats while providing a perfect marketing opportunity.

This site has regular special offers

Establishing your Web page background

The color and type of background you choose for your Web pages make a big difference to the impact your website makes. Here, we list the options and examine the benefits and drawbacks of using various types of background.

Covers

Chapter Three

Background: exotic or plain

The kind of background you choose for a Web page affects the readability of text more than any other single design trait. Always ensure that there is adequate color contrast between text and the Web page background and especially ensure physically challenged visitors can read your message more easily.

If you want to use a plain light-colored background but feel pure white is too "clinical" for your Web page content, consider creating an off-white color to considerably improve the warmth factor while at the same time helping make screen reading less dazzling.

Most people find that black text placed on a white or light background is easiest to read. Perhaps our eyes have become conditioned through books and newspapers. Whatever you decide, consider carefully any change that might interfere with legibility.

One of the most difficult combinations in which to achieve adequate contrast lies in using colored text on a colored background. Early browsers display a plain grey background; this is still the default for some AOL browser users. However, most newer browsers default to white. Therefore, always specify a background color using the BGROUND HTML tag. For example, the hexadecimal value – shown by the hash symbol # – of FFFFFF is pure white: <BODY BGCOLOR = "#FFFFFF">

Reading from a computer monitor demands more from the eye than when reading from paper-based documents. Don't use color combinations that make reading harder, such as: medium-dark colored text on a darker background.

You should decide what type of background is *appropriate*, bearing in mind the general content, image types and other components you want to overlay.

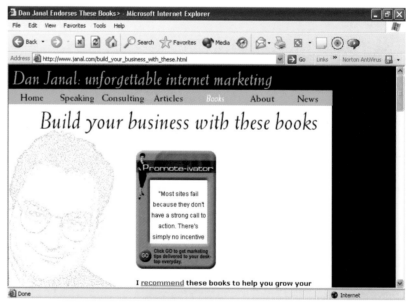

Pure black: a special approach

Skillfully done, a black background can be a powerful design trait to include in your Web page. Black enhances the sense of space and depth to a Web page. However, the use of such a large expanse of black needs careful consideration and good graphic design skills to succeed. Unless you're adept at this, stick to the more traditional presentation models of darker text on a lighter background.

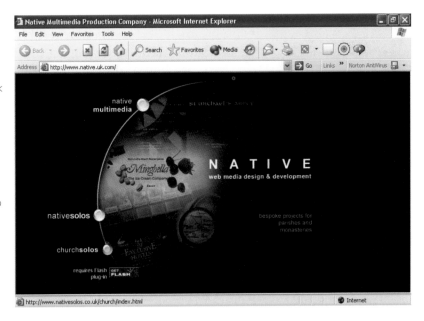

Colored text on a black background

Generally, people don't like to read a lot of text on a conventional screen: our eyes have to work harder than when reading from, say, paper. Recent studies also suggest that most people are not comfortable with white (or light colored) text on a black background. However, short one- or two-word titles, or yellow text on a black background, can provide excellent color contrast.

Images placed on a black background

Images placed on a black background can look either impressive or dreadful. If an image has not been designed for a black background, the results may be poor. However, when done properly the results can be stunning. For example, the black space used in the example demonstrates a high-order Web design brand perfectly.

Creating a picture background

Sometimes, you can enhance a Web page by using a single picture as the basis for the background. Consider the following guidelines:

A strong picture background probably works best in Web pages that contain limited amounts of text, or pages made primarily of graphical components.

- Use the <BODY BACKGROUND> HTML tag, HTML version 3.0 or later (see below).

- To ensure the picture is automatically tiled by the browser the image should be smaller than the browser window.

- Ensure the background does not overpower overlaying text. Convert the image to a light-colored watermark-type graphic. Embossing tones an image down yet ensures the essentials of the picture are still visible without interfering with the clarity of overlaid objects. See the example below:

If you decide to use an image in your page background, you should still always specify a background color so that those who turn images off see the color you intend. You can use the HTML <BGCOLOR> tag to meet this requirement.

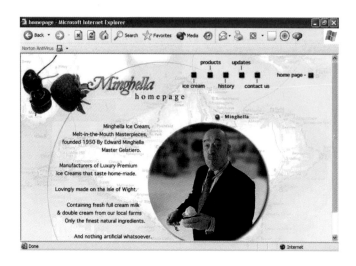

Creating a static background image

Normally, while you scroll down a page in a browser, the page content moves up. To make the background stationary, do this:

The stationary background effect outlined on the right usually works only in Microsoft Internet Explorer browsers, not Netscape.

1. A standard HTML background tag looks like this:

   `<BODY BACKGROUND="your_image.gif">`

2. Add the BGPROPERTIES tag like this:

   `<BODY BACKGROUND="your_image.gif" BGPROPERTIES="FIXED">`

Simple ways to create effective text

Words can make or break a website. The look and style of text you choose also have implications for your visitors. This chapter examines some of the best ways to create and display your text content.

Covers

Chapter Four

Providing what your visitors want

By ensuring your visitors know what to expect when they reach your Home/Index page, you can immediately build a temporary bond of trust, providing a kind of time margin – most people will suspend judgement until they get to know you better.

However, if your visitors expect to find information on a specific page but only find advertising, they may become irritated and start to lose faith in your site! For businesses, this is obviously bad news.

One way to ensure your Web pages display within an acceptable time frame is to try and ensure the text content on each page is restricted to fewer than about 600 words.

Make sure the text content of your Web pages provides all the *essential* points you want to put across: don't rely on graphical components to do this as some visitors may turn off graphics in their browser. However, remember: any brief key text message can also take the form of a graphic or be part of a Flash animation routine. You just need to ensure that each Web page can stand on its own and still make sense to visitors.

Be brief, simple, direct and sincere

Remember, most folks generally prefer to read long stretches of text from paper rather than from a display monitor. Therefore, consider the following guidelines:

You can make your Web pages printer-friendly by ensuring that the page width is not too wide, say under 550 pixels. However, remember: 550 pixels can look incredibly narrow on a larger display monitor. You won't please everyone, so make your best judgement. Experiment with different widths to ensure your visitors can view essential information when a page has been printed.

1 Keep your text content short, simple and relevant, using unambiguous words and phrases rather than long stretches of text. Use lots of surrounding space to frame text blocks.

2 Provide information in concise bursts: use short paragraphs of say 5 or 6 lines maximum.

3 Borrow ideas from the newspaper industry: consider using columns no wider than about 7 or 8 centimeters.

4 For longer sections of text, consider providing a brief introduction or outline, then include a link to the full version on another page. Visitors can then choose what they want quickly.

5 Read, then reread each line of text and remove all redundant words and phrases.

Working with fonts/typefaces

A font or typeface is a lettering style. You can choose which font styles you want to use in your pages by using any of the following design options:

- Use the fonts installed within the visitor's computer. For a visitor to see the exact same font you specify in your design, they'll need to also have the same font installed on their PC. If not, their Web browser chooses the next closest match.

- Convert the text you want to use to a graphic image.

- Create a Flash- or other animation-type sequence in which the desired font style is embedded within its own module.

Text components take up the least amount of file space compared to graphics, Flash animations and other elements.

When using pure text, design your pages using only fonts that are included as part of Microsoft Windows or the Apple Mac:

- Arial, Courier, Times Roman (for Windows PCs).

- Helvetica (for Apple Macs).

Also, Microsoft has created two excellent fonts designed especially for use on Web pages. Verdana and Georgia may be freely available for download from www.microsoft.com/ if they are not already included as part of your computer operating system.

In languages that read from left to right, body text is usually considered easier to read if aligned vertically at the left margin. This arrangement is sometimes referred to as being left-justified. Centered or right-justified text may be fine for the occasional heading if used sparingly. Try out several different combinations.

Using color and headings for exposure

In HTML, you can specify heading sizes easily: H1 (largest size), H2 (slightly smaller), and so on. For added contrast, consider using different colors for body text and headings.

Entering special characters

Often, you'll need to insert special characters/symbols that HTML reserves for its own use like the HTML "open tag" (<) and the ampersand (&) symbol. Or you may want to use characters not normally available from the keyboard, like the copyright symbol (©). If your Web design software does not already provide an easy way to enter these, simply type the symbols you want between the ampersand (&) and semicolon (;) symbols. For example:

- Less-than symbol (<), type: <

- Copyright symbol (©), type: ©

Top tips for working with text

1   Try to use fewer than three font styles. Why? Too many fonts can create a disjointed, "ransom note" effect.

You can "wrap" text around an image to provide an interesting effect. The HTML standard includes several attributes which let you do this by using the ALIGN =LEFT, =RIGHT, =TOP, =BOTTOM, and =CENTER attributes. See your HTML guide or "HTML in easy steps" for more details.

2   Headings: consider using a non-serif-type font, like Arial, Verdana, Helvetica or Georgia. Non-serif fonts don't have tails on letters.

3   Body text: consider using a serif typeface like Times Roman. Serif fonts are arguably easier to read at smaller sizes on a PC screen.

4   However, experiment! Try reversing your options. At the smaller fonts sizes of say 10p, Verdana and Georgia can excel.

5   To create an exotic or unusual font style, convert each desired text phrase/heading to a graphic (see Chapter 7 for details).

Microsoft created two excellent fonts designed to provide maximum readability on the Web: Verdana and Georgia. Therefore, why not make use of this valuable research?

6   Don't <u>underline</u> text just to add emphasis (unless it's a hyperlink). Instead consider using *italics* or **boldface** formatting instead.

7   Ensure headings make sense at a glance, or stimulate the reader's curiosity to discover more. Most people read headings first.

Working with hyperlinks

What gives the Web its enormous power is the ability to link to other pages and websites anywhere, in seconds. In this chapter, you can learn how to create text and graphical links between your pages and those of other websites.

Covers

Chapter Five

Text and graphical hyperlinks

A hyperlink is a link to another page or location in your website or to another page or location on the Web. You can create links with text or graphics. In fact, icons (small graphics) and buttons make ideal graphical links as they're usually physically small, and optimized for the Web, so can load quickly in a visitor's browser.

1 In this example, as the mouse is placed on a hyperlink button....

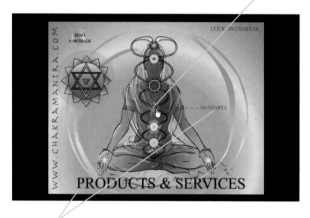

Many Web designers opt not to place the main site links on the right side of the page. However, for most search engines, this is THE ideal location, as a Search robot usually doesn't need to navigate through nonessential items (and JavaScript that may be confusing) before finding the important text for the page.

2 ... the text here changes to show what the active button refers to.

Whatever tool you use, a text HTML hyperlink usually takes the following basic form:

<A HREF="http://www.websitename.com/page.html"> Click here</A>

In the above example, a visitor would see only the words "Click here" usually underlined in blue to indicate that this text is a hyperlink. If you provide carefully considered links in your website, visitors don't have to use their browser Forward and Back buttons. Consider the following guidelines:

1 Ideally, place the main links to all other pages in your site at the top, left, bottom or right of all your pages – be consistent.

2 Make sure text hyperlinks especially are clearly visible against the page background. In later versions of HTML, you can change the look of text hyperlinks (see the facing page).

Creating hyperlinks that don't have underlines

By default, in most early Web page design HTML, hyperlinks are usually shown colored blue and underlined.

However, Web design has moved on and now more interesting options and alternatives are available to build more creative results.

If you want to be more creative, you can use Cascading Style Sheets (CSS) to create text links that are not underlined or which behave differently (see page 35 for details).

For now, here's a quick and easy way to create hyperlinks that don't have underlines:

1 Between your Web pages's <HEAD> and </HEAD> HTML tags, type in the following script exactly as it is displayed here. Note the { and } style brackets.

2 <STYLE TYPE="text/css">

<!—

a {text-decoration: none}

—>

</STYLE>

Creating hyperlink page bookmarks

Sometimes, you may want to provide a link to another location on the same Web page, rather than to another Web page or another location on the Net. You can do this by installing a bookmark (or intra-page) link. Here's how:

1 Place the insertion point where you want to create your bookmark and give the location a name in HTML. Example:

```
<A NAME="pagetop"></A>
```

2 Now move the insertion point to where you want to place your link then add the other half of the bookmark code:

```
<A HREF="#pagetop">Top of page.</A>
```

When a user clicks on "Top of page", they are returned to where the "pagetop" bookmark has been created. Alternatively, you can simply create a "jump-to-the-top-of-the-page-link" using this slightly different code: <a href="#" target="_top"> as shown in the example below created in Dreamweaver:

You can also open new windows using JavaScript code. Most modern Web browsers can interpret JavaScript easily. See your JavaScript guide for details. You can also learn more about JavaScript by reading "JavaScript in easy steps".

Example:

1 Fast-loading bookmark button.

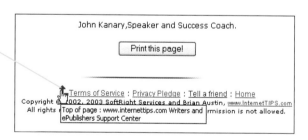

John Kanary,Speaker and Success Coach.

Print this page!

Terms of Service : Privacy Pledge : Tell a friend : Home
Copyright © 2002, 2003 SoftRight Services and Brian Austin, www.InternetTIPS.com
All rights Top of page : www.internettips.com Writers and rmission is not allowed.
ePublishers Support Center

```
<link rel="stylesheet" href="template3a.css" type="text/css">
<form class="body">
  <div align="center">
    <input type="button"
value="Print this page!"
onClick="javascript:print()">
  </div>
      </form><!-- #EndLibraryItem --><!-- #BeginLibraryItem "/Library/Copyright 2002
<div align="center">
  <p class="body"><img src="images/body_separator.gif" width="462" height="28" alt="body_s
  <a href="#" target="_top"><img src="images/page-top-blue.gif" width="18" height="16" a
  of service</a> : <a href="privacy/privacy-pledge.html">Privacy Pledge</a>
  : <a href="mailto:your-friend@email-address.com?subject=Check%20out%20this%20website&c
  a friend</a> : <a href="index.html">Home</a><font size="1"><br>
```

2 Here's the equivalent HTML.

Linking without losing your visitor

Once a visitor clicks a link to move to a new Web page, the usual way they can return to the same page is to simply click the browser Back button. However sometimes, you may prefer to keep the current Web page visible to your visitor for marketing purposes, and so forth. Web design tools like Dreamweaver and NetObjects Fusion enable you to arrange for a new, smaller browser window to open and which is overlaid on the current Web page window.

1 In this example, if this button link is clicked...

2 ...a new, smaller browser windows displays.

By arranging your design to open a second browser window, the original window stays visible and available, maintaining the connection to the starting focal point.

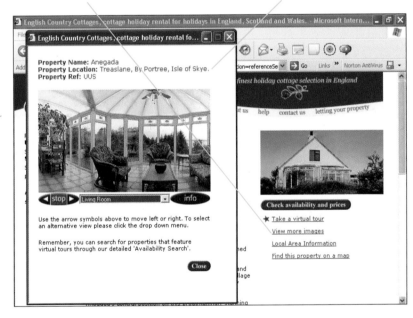

This snippet usually works on a "live" Web page. Edit the text into a "test" page and publish it to the Web before adapting for your live page.

Creating a link to open a visitor's mailbox

Add the following snippet of code to provide a link on a page that when clicked can open a visitor's mailbox (this should work fine on most recent Web browsers):

```
<A HREF="mailbox:Inbox">Click To Open Your Mailbox</A>
```

You could replace the text: "Click To Open Your Mailbox" with a graphic icon, or button if you prefer.

Linking back to the Home/Index page

Always include a link back to your Home/Index page on all other pages in your site, to provide visitors with a quick way to get back to the start with a single click. A logo can make an ideal Home link.

While viewing a page in your website, visitors may suddenly decide to contact you. This is good: never make it hard for them. You could ensure ease of access by including a link to your "Contacts" page or "Feedback" section on every page in your website.

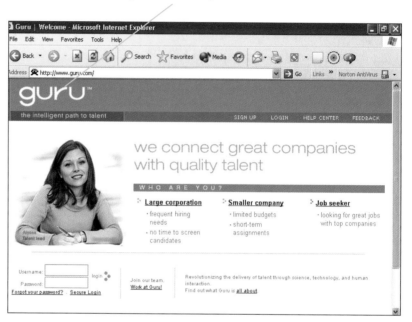

Sending visitors to a new Home/Index page

Often, you may want to create a new website while keeping an old website operational for a while. Here's how to redirect visitors to the new site Home/Index page:

1 In the "old" Home/Index page, add the following code between the <HEAD> and </HEAD> tags:

<META HTTP-EQUIV="Refresh" CONTENT="5" URL="http://www.yourcompany.com/newpage.htm">

In this example, we've arranged for a visitor to be redirected to the new page in 5 seconds (CONTENT=5). If you want a different value, simply change this "CONTENT" value to the number you want.

2 For the "URL=..." section in Step 1, substitute with the new Web address you want to use.

3 You may also want to create a normal text link to the new Home page to allow for older browsers.

4 Save the updated page, publish to the Web and test.

Working with related websites

Providing a link to other websites might not, at first, seem like an effective way of enhancing your own Web pages. However, this method can be a very effective way to increase your website's ranking in the search engines, or boost your site's popularity.

Three or more websites could even work together to provide special deals for customers and to help boost each member's own individual product sales. Joint venturing in this way can immensely benefit all, providing all partners cooperate equally.

Let's assume you provide a website selling books. You could include a link to another online store that sells videos and music CDs. Imagine a music celebrity has just published their sizzling autobiography; after customers have ordered their book on your Web order form, they could also easily gain access to our celebrity's most popular videos/CDs simply by clicking the associated link. They're already in a buying mood and that's the best time to make an additional related offer.

Customers benefit by having access to a better service and to related subjects if they choose to follow these up. Likewise, the video website provider could include a complementary link to the bookseller's Home page. Both Web providers can benefit from new visitors. Here's one strategy to consider:

FFA (Free-For-All) pages are provided by other websites who let you announce your Web page address for free. In return, they get more visitors to their site. If you decide to submit your site to FFA pages, use a spare, disposable email address, not your main email address, to avoid getting lots of spam (unwanted) email messages as a result.

1 Locate names of complementary organizations that you would like to be associated with. Search engines can be useful here to find exact Web addresses.

2 Contact each of these chosen sites, send a brief email to the Webmaster introducing yourself, your website and your proposal. Mention that in return for them including a link to your website, you will include a link to theirs.

3 If agreement is reached, you can include an eye-catching attractive link either on a dedicated "Other links" page, or another appropriate page.

4 Try to win some site awards – or create your own Awards page.

5 Consider adding your website address to as many Free For All (FFA) pages as you consider appropriate (but see the DON'T FORGET tip).

Top tips for superb linking

Creating a hyperlink in HTML is not difficult. However, creating a linking structure that is simple, efficient and pleases both your visitors and the search engines is more challenging. Consider the following tips:

LinkBot is a service that can check all the links in your site for you. A really useful tool. To discover more, point your browser at: www. linkbot.com/

1 Use HTML tables to align your links neatly on the page.

2 Make sure all links are correct, work properly and are up-to-date.

3 Make your site easy to navigate on all pages. Ideally, create a familiar style that visitors can immediately identify with.

4 Don't force visitors into a specific way of navigation: provide several alternative pathways to the same information and let your visitors decide the route they want to take.

5 Don't rely on graphical links only. Provide equivalent text and links on each page (also used by search engine spiders).

6 Remember, visitors may enter your site via pages other than your main access pages: provide hierarchical links so that your visitors can move to any other page in your site using fewer than four mouse clicks (three is better).

7 If your site has many pages – say over 50 – consider adding a Sitemap page to help visitors quickly find their way.

8 To create a standalone link that does not have the default underline, add the STYLE="text-decoration:none" attribute to the tag. For example:

<A HREF="http://yourcompany.com/gold.html"

STYLE="text-decoration:none">Click Here for this week's gold offer</A>

Developing your website colors

Color is everywhere. Color is awesome. It can bring things to life, entice us, steal our attention, trigger pleasurable emotional responses or make us reel with disgust! Use of color in your website is governed by the same rules. Let's explore what we can do with color to make your Web pages a runaway success.

Covers

Chapter Six

Colors and color combinations

Different colors can mean different things to different people. Colors are used as labels and some color combinations have special significance in some cultures, so beware! Consider the following guidelines typical in Western culture:

- Red, yellow and orange can be considered attention-getting, exciting or warning-type colors.

- Green inspires hope and suggests renewal. It's also a reliable, relaxing, earthy color closely associated with life.

- Strong blue is often linked to trust, providing a hint as to why we so often see blue used in corporate stationery. In another context, blue can also be considered cold, calm or tranquil depending on the intended mood.

Be especially careful with the use of the HTML <BLINK> tag combined with red text. This is an alarming combination; make sure that is what you want to achieve.

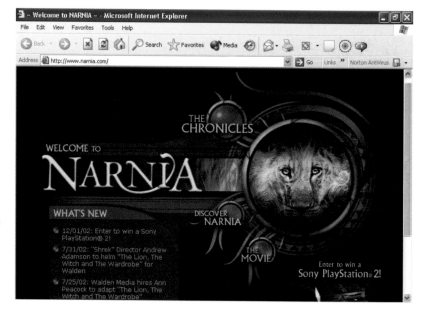

Color Schemer is low-priced shareware that lets you try out different color mixes, and helps you choose combinations that work well together on the Web. For more information, visit: www. colorschemer.com/.

- Black can suggest space, contrast, depth and the mysterious. White can also help create the illusion of space and is often linked to cleanliness, sterility, purity or innocence.

- Purple and magenta evoke a rich, regal tone of nobility and ceremony. They can also suggest wisdom, transformation, enlightenment, even cruelty and arrogance.

Creating adequate contrast

A color may be considered "bright", but when that same color is overlaid on another, the perception may be entirely different. Good contrast between a colored object and the color of the space surrounding it is an essential aspect for clear Web page design. Through learning and mastering powerful graphics software, a Web designer can create beautiful artistic creations in their own right which engage the visitor, enchant, and stimulate interest.

If you're developing a new adventurous Web color scheme, get feedback from others (at an early stage) to gauge opinions on how it is accepted. Feel free to explore the boundaries and try new approaches. Isn't that how all progress is made?

Thinking about the color of text

Results of recent scientific legibility studies have shown that, when reading, most people prefer to view black text on a white background. White text placed on a black background is often considered the least preferred option as it is generally held to be the environment in which text is hardest to read – especially on a computer display monitor.

However, this combination may work better when keeping to larger typeface sizes of the sort used for headings, or text blocks which include only a few words. Perhaps the best advice is to produce your own trial pages and examine closely the issue of text legibility, particularly in relation to text color and background combinations.

Top Web color hints and tips

1 Develop a color scheme that does not interfere with the main message of your Web page and use it consistently.

Most display monitors can now display a minimum of 256 colors – 40 of which are used by the PC's operating system, leaving 216 "Web safe" colors. Any color from the 216-color palette will always display correctly using Microsoft Internet Explorer, Netscape Navigator and other compatible browsers on all current operating systems.

2 If you want to define your own colors, ideally keep to the 216-color palette (see the DON'T FORGET tip), but keep to 256 colors, or greater, for photos.

3 Avoid overusing color. The best way to meet this goal is to have a concrete and justifiable reason for using each color.

4 Use adventurous color combinations with care. Bright neon green on bright orange makes quite an impact on the eye. This may be fine if your visitors might expect such a combination at your website, but is less likely to be suitable for, say, an information-dominated website.

5 Consider carefully whether you should use more than 2 or 3 colors for your main body text and headings.

Some argue that specific website color combinations – like neon green on a purple backdrop, for example – can cause headaches amongst some viewers.

6 An attention-grabbing color can only grab attention if used selectively. Setting all the body text in red lessens the impact red makes. Instead, carefully choose key words or short phrases for highlighting in one form or another.

7 Color is a kind of signpost – use it in a consistent way so visitors soon get to know what a specific color on your website means. This concept is particularly important for navigation links etc.

8 Consider those visitors who might be color-blind. A color-blind visitor may become one of your most lucrative customers, but only if he or she can see what you're offering. Take a little time to learn about color blindness. Red and green appear the same to color-blind folks. Create clear color contrast between text and background.

How to create stunning Web graphics

Pictures, images and photos can add interest and attraction to a Web page. Often, the most striking Web pages make good use of carefully designed images. This chapter introduces current Web image formats and explains how to create stunning images.

Covers

Chapter Seven

Introducing Web graphics

"A picture speaks a thousand words"! On the Web, carefully considered pictures, graphics and animations can do just that. You can enrich a plain page with maps, cartoons, diagrams, photographs and attractive button-type icons for site navigation and other purposes. Navigation toolbars are particularly popular. However, images must be converted and optimized before use on a Web page to ensure they load quickly and can be viewed by your visitors. Current types of Web image are examined in the following pages.

How your display monitor creates an image

An image on a monitor is made up of thousands of dots of light or pixels. Many current monitors can display an area 800 x 600 pixels resolution, which means 800 pixels wide by 600 pixels high. Other resolutions include the older 640 x 480 and the now more common 1024 x 768 which is best used on larger screen sizes.

1024 x 768

800 x 600

640 x 480

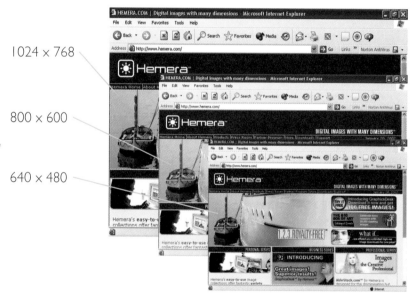

Creating simple navigational aids

Lots of attractive, interesting and complex images are available. But for site navigation and page layout, simple graphics are usually the best choice. A horizontal rule, for example, is an ideal fast-loading layout aid to use when you want to separate blocks of text by subject matter or topic. "Simplicity" has a power of its own sometimes.

Web image types

All sorts of graphics can be included in a Web page and a wide range of image types are already available for use in all sorts of documents. For example, you may have heard of terms like BMP, CGM, PCX, TIF, WMF, GIF, JPG and (more recently) PNG. The ending given to the name of an image shows what type of graphic is being used. So, for example, the file SEASCAPE.JPG tells us that "seascape" is a JPG-type image.

Usually, to ensure fast page loading, Web images should be converted to one of the following formats (developed specifically for onscreen/online use):

Not only can pictures help make a Web page more interesting, they can help break down the language barrier for visitors whose native language is not your own. The correct picture really can substitute for a thousand words.

- GIF (Graphics Interchange Format).

- JPEG (Joint Photographic Experts Group format).

- PNG (Portable Network Graphics format).

What's in a GIF?

The GIF or Graphics Interchange Format is ideal for simple Web graphics containing a low number of colors such as some logos, icons, buttons, maps and ornate lines. A GIF image is made up of pixels (see the facing page). The color of each pixel contributes to the colors used in the entire image.

You can include graphics other than GIF, JPEG or PNG in your Web pages by utilizing "plug-in" technology. However, there's little need to do so, and you would then have to ensure your visitors have the correct plug-in installed. In most instances, the best route is to simply convert the image you want to GIF or JPEG.

High-quality rollover graphics in the award-winning www.escapetotheedge.com

The GIF format filters out unnecessary information to provide a compact image file size. The maximum number of colors to use in a Web GIF is 256 – fine for many images but not usually for photos. A series of GIFs can be combined to create a moving image sequence almost like a small movie to create a dynamic or animated-GIF (animation is covered in Chapter 10). A GIF can also have a transparent background, useful if you're using a particular background image in a Web page.

If you use a scanner to capture images for use on the Web, ideally set the resolution to 100% and scan at 72–75 dpi. To keep image size low, crop non-essential parts.

JPEG – the photographic format

More complex images than simple logos may be best saved in JPEG format. Joint Photographic Experts Group is ideal for displaying photographic Web images. Here are the key traits:

- JPEG files have the filename extension .jpg.

- Like GIF, JPEG is a high compression format and uses up to about 16.7 million colors.

- However, JPEG files don't usually convert small typefaces, solid image blocks or hard lines as well as the GIF format.

The PNG graphics format

A more recent addition to the Web graphics format gallery, Portable Network Graphics (PNG) is another high-compression format ideal for use on the Web. One of PNG's most striking and potentially powerful features is that these images can contain embedded textual information (Meta-tags) that can be detected by the Internet search engines. However, different PNG file types can exist for both the PC and the Apple Mac. PNG images designed for one platform may not display at their best on the other.

Preparing images for the Web

Copyright and legal issues

All images are intellectual property. Before using any graphics or other content that you do not own, get written permission from the copyright owner to use them in your Web pages.

Digital watermarking an image

To apply copyright to an image, you can embed a digital watermark into the image. DigiMarc is one established organization providing digital watermarking software. Point your browser at: www. digimarc.com for more information:

More recent versions of Adobe Photoshop provide an easy-to-use command to insert a DigiMarc watermark into an image.

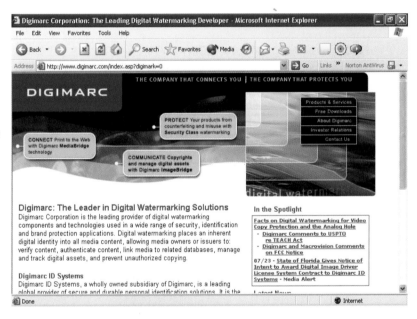

Disabling browser "Save image..." mouse commands

If you want to apply some quick direct protection from visitors "borrowing" images from your site, here's one option to consider. The following (currently free) script disables the right mouse button image Save commands in Microsoft Internet Explorer v4.x and Netscape Navigator v4.x and all later browsers. The script may not currently work with Apple Mac PCs and is not a complete solution (more knowledgeable users can still find your images in their browser cache folders, for example):

http://javascript.internet.com/page-details/no-right-click.html

Optimizing images for Web use:

1 To create and prepare your images, use suitable Web graphics-editing software like Paint Shop Pro and make sure you choose the Red, Green and Blue (RGB) color mode.

2 Make any edits to your images only at high color depths (16 million colors) and larger physical sizes.

3 When ready to place an image on a Web page, make a copy then reduce the physical size of the copy to the size you want.

4 Reduce the color depth of the images to a suitable level: GIF – 256 or 16 colors; JPG – keep to 16 million colors.

5 One of the most important Web image characteristics is the file size or Kb value. Kb is short for Kilobyte, (2^{10} or 1024 bytes). In Windows Explorer, with the View>Details command active, you can see the Kb size of any highlighted image. Aim to get this figure as low as possible but without sacrificing image quality.

Interlacing images

Download time for a 40K or more standard GIF image (GIF-87a) can sometimes seem too long. Interlacing allows larger capacity images to appear to be displayed quicker. A visitor can see a low quality definition image (GIF-89a) before it is fully defined.

Interlacing splits an image file into two sets of alternate bands. While the image downloads on a visitor's browser, one set of bands is displayed first – at this stage of the image download, the entire image is visible but indistinct.

Only when the other set of bands is fully downloaded is the full image clearly visible. If you want to provide a suspense or surprise element, a non-interlaced GIF-89a may offer a better choice.

Creating an interlaced GIF

When using a logo on a Web page, convert the logo file to GIF format (unless your logo is particularly complex, in which case consider using JPEG or PNG instead). Compare file sizes and choose the most appropriate format. Alternatively, good quality graphics software, like Photoshop and Fireworks, can suggest the best solution.

You can easily create an interlaced GIF-89a format from a non-interlaced GIF or from many standard image formats using the appropriate commands in any suitable image editing program such as Paint Shop Pro, Adobe Photoshop or GIF Lube at: www.websitegarage.com/.

Progressive JPEG – a similar approach

Ordinary JPEG images can't be interlaced. However, Progressive JPEG – a more recent development of the JPEG standard – provides a similar feature.

When a progressive JPEG image downloads, an approximation of the image is displayed on the first cycle with further details added on subsequent cycles until finally the entire image at its full resolution is displayed.

Creating transparent images

Sometimes, you may want to place an image on a Web page but without keeping the default image background; you may already have decided to use a specific page background and want that to show through instead giving the impression that the image is transparent.

Of the two main image formats examined on previous pages, currently only the GIF-89a format supports image transparency.

How to create a transparent image

GIF-89a provides additional features over and above those available for GIF-87a, one of which is image transparency.

You can create a transparent GIF-89a by modifying an existing GIF-87a or creating an entirely new image using a suitable application, like Paint Shop Pro. The GIF Construction Set from Alchemy Mindworks is another well known shareware application from which you can create transparent GIFs (also animated or dynamic GIFs as outlined in Chapter 10). For more information, visit: www.mindworkshop.com/alchemy/alchemy.html

Transparent GIFs help create attractive, stunning graphics

Setting optimal image size

While preparing graphics in conversion programs like Paint Shop Pro and Adobe Photoshop, you may be given a choice of palettes. Usually, if possible, you'll want to choose Adaptive or Optimized at the conversion stage if you want to get as close a match as possible to the original image.

Using pictures and other graphics in Web pages has implications that you should be aware of when considering your overall page design. One of the most important aspects is the file size of every image or graphic used. By file size, essentially we're referring to the combination of the number of colors used – or color depth – as well as the physical size. Color depth is covered overleaf.

The physical size of an image is determined by its horizontal and vertical dimensions. Physical size (combined with other factors) determines the image file size. One benchmark to consider, is to try and make each image in your Web page use fewer than about 20–30 Kb. However, now that Internet access speeds are increasing, larger images can sometimes offer the best choice if you consider the impact and presentation are worth the trade off.

Considering download time

The larger the image, the longer it takes to download. Even a small thumbprint image can use many thousands of Kilobytes if not correctly optimized. If a Web page contains multiple images, download time increases correspondingly.

A carefully prepared "focal point" image can make a big impact

Establishing ideal color depth

Color depth describes how many colors are used to make up an image. While a GIF image may adequately display using 256 colors, photos usually display poorly at this level. For photos, 64K or even 16 million colors would probably provide best results.

Aim to keep the color depth as low as possible for the image you're using. That is either 16 or 256 colors for GIFs and 32,768 or 65,536 colors for JPEGs.

However, do let the image quality and its central purpose dictate the lowest setting you should use. Why? If you reduce the color depth for an image too much, the image can appear jagged and patchy, as shown in the leftmost example at the bottom of the page.

We can also describe color depth in terms of bits instead of colors. The following table illustrates how color and bit depth are related:

Number of colors	Bit depth
2 colors	1-bit
16 colors	4-bit
256 colors	8-bit
32,768 colors	16-bit
65,536 colors	Also 16-bit
16,777, 216 colors	24-bit or 32-bit

The photo opposite is borrowed (copyright courtesy of Neil Smith, www.latitude57.co.uk). The author has manipulated the example image to demonstrate different resolutions. The genuine image is high quality. You can view more great images and informative multimedia CD-ROMs about Skye and Scotland at the above address.

16 colors (JPEG)   256 colors (JPEG)   16 million colors (JPEG)

Using thumbnail images

A thumbnail image is a small "preview" representation of the "real" full-size image. As a thumbnail image is smaller, it downloads much quicker than the "main" image and so is an ideal way to reduce download time while still providing the essential content.

When visitors want to see the main image, they simply click the thumbnail to open a new window containing the full size image.

Try to avoid including large photographic-type images in your Web pages. A large photograph could take up two or more megabytes: this can take quite a while to download, especially when using slower modem connection speeds.

PictureDicer is a freeware program that can chop a large graphic into smaller sections for speedier downloading and arrange the sections into a neat table. For more information, visit: www.ziplink.net/~shoestring/dicer01.htm.

With thumbnails, visitors can choose what to view in detail, rather than having to endure longer download times for irrelevant information. Thumbnail images are ideal when an associated "main" image is a larger, high- resolution, photographic-type image (using the JPEG format).

Thumbnail images demonstrate consideration for your visitors who will most likely have cause to remember such thoughtfulness.

An important point about thumbnail images is that they introduce choice to your visitor. The best advice is to never provide direct access to any large, photographic-type images: try to provide a thumbnail stand-in and let your visitors decide what to download.

Providing impact with imagemaps

An imagemap is a single, usually larger than "normal" image that contains two or more links to other Web pages in the current site or to other Web addresses (URLs).

Each specific area of an imagemap or "hotspot" is assigned a different link address. A visitor simply clicks the desired hotspot to jump to another Web page or Web address. These defined areas can be irregular in shape or have a more common profile like a button or icon.

Imagemaps can result in larger file sizes than you might expect. Therefore, this is an area for the Web page designer to watch.

An imagemap is a neat way of including multiple links in a small space. Picture imagemaps are often used as an attractive alternative to a conventional button menu of links.

Always include equivalent text links in an imagemap, to ensure some information is still available even if visitors have turned off graphics in their browsers.

An imagemap can only be detected by a graphically activated Web browser, not one that is text-based or has graphics detection turned off.

In this imagemap example from NetObjects Fusion, these areas are defined as hotspots/hyperlinks

You can include an imagemap in a Web page in two ways: client-side or – more rarely nowadays – server-side. Both methods have benefits and drawbacks. However, with a little more work, you can provide the best option by combining both techniques. See your HTML guide for full details.

Creating an imagemap

The better graphical Web design software packages like FrontPage and NetObjects Fusion provide simple commands to create and fine-tune imagemaps or you can use one of the many special applications designed for the job. Your browser search facilities can help you find one.

Including ALT tags

For every image you use, make sure you include the necessary HTML ALT code to provide a text marker equivalent. Here's why:

- Some visitors may disable the graphics capabilities of their browsers to speed up page download time. ALT tags help make sense of the page.

- If a search engine scans your website while regularly "spidering" the Web, carefully created text markers for all graphics can sometimes increase your page ranking.

- Some disabled visitors may not be able to view your graphics. Text equivalents can help make sense of a Web page. Some electronic readers can also identify ALT tags.

Here's an example of the use of the ALT tag:

```
<IMG SRC="ahlogo.gif" HEIGHT=50 WIDTH=200 ALT="Austin Hall logo">
```

You can use single words, phrases and even brief sentences in ALT text descriptions. These can be carefully worded to maximize specific search engine requirements and ranking (Chapter 13). For example, the flagged text describes the image precisely.

Many Internet search engines regularly scan or "spider" the Web to update their records and find websites to include in their indexes. They'll often detect ALT tags if they're available. Also possible: some search engines and directories may penalize sites that do not have ALT tags for all images.

Web graphics round-up: 10 top tips

1 Don't fall into the common trap of including too many graphics and text in a space. If necessary, break up a page into multiple pages. Then, information is easier to read and pages load faster, further enhancing your visitors' experience.

2 On Web pages, images are best measured in pixels. So for Web design, think in terms of pixels (shown in the Step 3 example) rather than centimeters.

Like cartoons, line art images (with the addition of a little color) can translate well onto a website. Line art images also compress easily and quickly. However, perhaps most useful from a Web design aspect is their simplicity. A simple illustration often stands out from the rest.

3 Use the <WIDTH> and <HEIGHT> HTML tags to help images load in a browser quicker (usually):

<IMG SRC="image.gif" WIDTH=50 HEIGHT=25>

4 For each image or graphic you use, aim to create the smallest graphics file for the best image quality possible.

5 Include a brief text equivalent description using the HTML <ALT> tag for each graphic used.

6 Try to keep photographic-type images to less than 200 pixels horizontally and vertically to reduce time needed to download.

Don't put larger images at the top of a Home/Index page. Some visitors may not wait for them to download; if so, you've probably lost them permanently!

7 To reduce page download time, keep the total graphics content of each page to less than about 50 Kb maximum and reuse the same images wherever possible.

8 Colorful and complex is not always best. Simple line art images, like those found in newspaper cartoons, can sometimes be just as effective as more elaborate images.

9 The Web is essentially a graphical medium so, wherever appropriate, use attractive images on your Web pages. Pictures/graphics are usually better than lots of text – and are usually more interesting from a visitor's viewpoint.

10 Use "active" empty space to frame your content.

Designing frame-based Web pages

Creating Web pages using frames is like placing several Web pages into a single window. Sounds great, doesn't it? However, there are pitfalls. Here, you can learn how best to use frames in your Web pages.

Covers

Chapter Eight

Introducing frames

With frames, you can arrange for a desired section of a Web page to stay the same while other parts may change as a visitor navigates. Most current browsers can display framed websites adequately.

Arguably, a framed website is harder for a search engine spidering program to index. If a higher ranking in the search engine directories is important, consider your framed design carefully to maximize positive results. Better still, in the author's opinion, simply don't use frames in these instances.

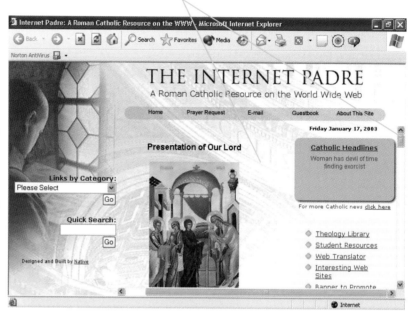

How it all works

A "normal" HTML Web document uses the <BODY> </BODY> HTML tag-pair. In a framed Web page, the <FRAMESET> </FRAMESET> tag-pair is used in place of the <BODY> tags.

In a framed website, the Frameset document needs to download only once to a visitor's browser. As the visitor navigates through the various pages in a site, only the changing content pages need downloading. If you don't want to get too involved with the HTML syntax, most DTP-based Web design software packages provide easy commands to create framed websites/pages.

The reason why multiple frames can be an advertiser's best friend

In Web pages that are essentially advertising-driven, frames can be particularly valuable. You can set up your design so that a banner, advertising slogan, or compelling animation is held in place while a visitor navigates in the adjacent frames.

Frame types

You can use a variety of frame options in your Web pages:

- **Basic frames** – set up areas of the screen with standard borders by default. A variety of attributes can be applied.

- **Multiple frames** – several frames are possible.

- **Floating frames** – provides for frames that can be sited anywhere in the browser window.

- **Linking frames** – enables a visitor to click on a link in one frame (say one of a list of buttons) to cause the content of another linked frame to change.

- **Borderless frames** – available with later versions of Netscape Navigator/Communicator and Microsoft's Internet Explorer. Can help produce some snappy results.

- **Frames containing custom borders** – a Microsoft Internet Explorer enhancement. Lets you specify background colors.

In HTML you can establish frame sizes using the number of rows, columns, percentages or pixels.

Don't design a framed website that forces a visitor to scroll from left to right to read the page content. This effect will almost certainly irritate visitors; some simply won't put up with it and move to another easier site. You'll almost certainly never see that visitor again.

Using frames in a Web page

Deciding whether to use frames is often not as simple as it may first appear and so needs careful consideration. For some applications, frames can save huge amounts of time. However, some users simply don't like them. Let's take a closer look and examine some of the benefits and drawbacks:

A separate frame can sometimes provide an ideal "container" for a rotating banner advert or animated Java-type news component.

Benefits:

- Each frame can be considered to be a separate window and as such can contain a completely separate HTML document.

- A "fixed" frame is an ideal container into which you can place items that normally would not change from page to page. These items include logos, marketing messages, toolbars or standard button links.

- Frames can help provide a kind of grand tour of a range of products, website, building, and so on.

- Frame links can be tied together so that carrying out an action in one frame can cause changes to occur in another frame. Some spectacular effects can be achieved using this technique.

- A frame can include a border that is displayed or hidden. Multiple frames with hidden borders, with each frame containing its own active content, can help create some compelling and spectacular effects.

Drawbacks:

- Frames usually take longer to download; you need to be sure this will be tolerated by your visitors.

- Having several active frames makes things more hectic and may confuse visitors or blur the main message of the page.

- Framed websites usually make search engine spidering programs work harder, to say the least.

- Not all browsers can deal with frames. Ideally, you may also have to include an equivalent "frameless" version for those visitors who require it.

Hands-on action guidelines

Consider the following guidelines for deciding whether to use frames and, if so, how to ensure you have a trouble-free frame experience in Web design:

Test your new framed Web page designs using several different Web browsers to ensure you get the results you expect.

1 Too many frames can cause confusion and lengthen download times. Keep to no more than 3 frames, unless you have a compelling, convincing reason to include a fourth.

2 Working with frames in HTML is harder than working with non-framed pages. Frames can be troublesome. Poor frame designs can be a nightmare!

3 Some older browsers can't understand frames. Even today, visitors with these browsers may feel alienated unless you provide non-framed pages also. However, this dual approach can double your workload and significantly increase the amount of time spent maintaining and updating your pages.

4 With frames, it's easy to end up making too much information available to a visitor at the same time, causing confusion and conflict between different elements. Your central message may then be missed by your visitors.

5 Place the HTML <NOFRAMES> and </NOFRAMES> tag-pair into the Frameset document to enter information, search engine key words and meta tags that only frame-incompatible browsers will see. Careful choices here can help improve your site's ranking in some search engines.

A browser's Back button may not work properly when viewing a framed website.

6 If possible, include a component that tests whether a visitor is using a frame-enabled browser and, if not, arrange for a statement to be displayed on the screen stating that fact: *"This site/page uses frames but your browser either doesn't support them or has frames turned off".*

Helping visitors break out of frames

If you're not using frames in your Web design, sometimes a visitor may log onto your site still trapped in a frame from visiting a previously framed website.

The drawback from this condition is that they may see the address or URL of the previously visited website in their browser's Location/Address box while viewing and navigating your website.

This is one result you probably don't want – especially if you're in business. You can just never know: the previous website could be your main competitor, ouch!

So what can you do? Fear not, here's some simple JavaScript code that you can enter into your Web page to help your visitor break free and return their browser to its normal condition:

Don't use this "break-out" script if you're using frames in your own Web pages.

1. Insert the following code as high as possible between the \<HEAD> and \</HEAD> tags in your HTML so that the script will run before your page has fully downloaded:

2. Text

```
<SCRIPT LANGUAGE="JavaScript">

<!— Start

if (parent.location.href != window.location.href)

parent.location.href = window.location.href

// — End —>

</SCRIPT>
```

If you're serious about creating some neat special effects in your Web pages, deciding to take some time to learn the basics of JavaScript is always a worthwhile investment.

You can learn more about JavaScript – and have some fun – from the companion book in this series: "JavaScript in easy steps".

Including audio in your website

The ability to include background sounds, voices and music adds a whole new dimension to a website. This chapter explains the basics, shows how to include sound components and explores the latest techniques.

Covers

Chapter Nine

The basics of audio on the Web

Sound offers the Web page designer exciting possibilities. Audio can enliven a Web page and may be especially valuable for visitors with vision problems. Sometimes, a simple piece of music can single-handedly create in your visitor the mood you want to achieve. Also, unlike pictures that may need supporting text to make sense, sound and especially voice content can stand on its own without any further support being required.

Powerful reasons why sound can benefit a site

While perhaps viewing a page, a visitor could listen to a voice accompaniment. Even simple voice recordings could provide:

- Background, support, marketing or sales information.

- Help or assistance for visitors.

- Entertainment or samples to hear or download.

Microsoft Windows comes with the Sound Recorder utility. You can use Sound Recorder to record, play and edit any WAVe files you want to include in your Web pages. For more information, see your Windows documentation.

Web sound components come in two main flavors: digital or synthesized audio format. Often, providers of the various sound technologies make available free plug-ins for their particular sound technology. So what else is possible?

- Discrete sound clips: the relevant file must be fully downloaded before the sound component can play.

- Live audio streaming: a visitor can listen to the sound even while the relevant file is downloading.

- Live audio, talk shows, news, etc.: a visitor can hear what is being delivered as it actually happens.

What a visitor needs to hear Web sounds

To hear Web sounds, visitors must meet two conditions:

1. Their PC must contain the necessary sound hardware, either a sound card or sound chips installed directly onto the motherboard (plus speakers or at least headphones). Most PCs/Apple Macs now include sound support.

2. Their default browser must support the appropriate sound format being used or have the correct plug-in or helper application correctly installed and set up.

Popular sound formats

To use sound on a Web page, first the sound clips must be converted into an appropriate format. Current options include:

- WAVe format (.wav): compatible with both the Microsoft Windows and Apple Mac platforms.

- MIDI (.midi, .mid) Musical Instrument Digital Interface: used with musical instruments and synthesizers.

- AIFF (.aiff) Audio Interchange File Format: originally Apple Mac format, can also play on later Windows PCs with the correct plug-in installed.

- AU (.au) format: used in Java applets, NeXT systems and Sun Microsystems PCs.

- MPEG (.mpg): popular format used for Web video clips.

- RealAudio (.ra, .ram): popular for streaming (live continuous play) audio. Your Web host needs to be compatible. Visitors need the RA Player browser plug-in installed.

- MP3 (.mp3): also from the Motion Picture Expert Group, MP3 is now one of the most popular audio formats online.

Some of the latest presentation software packages include plug-ins that can enable a Web page provider to broadcast a presentation on the Web. To gain further information, check out the latest versions of Lotus Freelance Graphics and Microsoft PowerPoint.

MPEG stands for Motion Picture Expert Group (sometimes referred to as Moving Pictures Experts Group). The MPEG have been responsible for making available a range of popular file formats now used on the Internet, including: .mpg, .mpeg, .m1v, .mp2, .mp3, .mpa, and .mpe.

Exploring musical possibilities

Music can affect people in a variety of ways. If you want to put over a particular mood in a website, musical content can help considerably. Consider the basics:

- Fast, dynamic music emphasizes action, tension or excitement.

- Contrastingly of course, slow and lingering music can help evoke a feeling of calmness and relaxation.

- Also, the right kind of music for a website doesn't need any further explanation: music is its own language.

Longer musical sequences can put a greater strain on visitors' computer resources, whilst shorter bursts are less open to error and can sometimes be just as effective.

If you're trying to create a particular mood, the musical content of a Web page usually works best if the particular clip contains characteristics that make for a soothing and calming presentation, rather than one that is exciting or stirring.

Let's explore some ideas of the kinds of websites that might benefit from including music components:

- An English gardening site could include a few opening bars of an English dawn chorus carefully recorded at daybreak in springtime.

- A geographical website with an Australian interest could include a short sequence of an Aboriginal didgeridoo to evoke the mood of the outback.

- A corporate site could include a few confident, powerful and stimulating bars – just as the Home/Index page loads and the corporate logo emerges.

- Imagine a travel-based website is running a special holiday promotion to, say, Mexico. A few bars of traditional Mexican music can really set the scene as photos of Mexican culture and scenery are teased into view with the latest incredible travel offers temptingly woven into the presentation.

This way of thinking can be applied to any website theme and can enhance your presentation, leaving a memorable impression with your visitor. A perfect reason to revisit and stay in touch!

Installing sound on a Web page

Both music and voice accompaniments can be arranged to play when a Web page displays or when a visitor clicks a specific button or moves their mouse across a designated location on the screen.

"Humanizing" the Web

One of the most powerful aspects of voice recordings is the human element. Although the Web is a powerful medium, it still has an essentially electronic, distant "feel" to it. Contrastingly, the tonal highs and lows of a voice recording can put over personality and individuality. Arguably, the current general inhumanity of the commercial Web may have held back more rapid development and take up by higher numbers of visitors. People want to "connect" with other people, not to a faceless Internet.

Sound files can have copyright applied to them. If you use other people's material, get written permission first and always keep a copy.

However, visitors can become irritated if a recording plays for too long. Therefore, try to aim for the minimum time possible; have a specific purpose in mind and try to avoid cramming too much into the sound sequence.

Sound components installation

Here's a great idea for a personal Web page containing a CV that can really help you to get noticed. Amaze and impress prospective employers by including a carefully crafted optional RealAudio sound file with an embedded Start/Stop button. Let them know about you and sell yourself before you even get to the interview!

Using the correct HTML, you can embed sound components into a Web page or link them to it. Embedded sound components are usually downloaded automatically when a visitor logs on to a Web page. Linked sound components usually include control buttons to enable visitors to decide if they want to play the sequence.

WAVe files can be created easily using the Windows Sound Recorder utility. You can also create files in other formats using one of the many dedicated sound recorder applications available.

For visitors using Microsoft Internet Explorer browsers, sound files installed using the HTML <BGSOUND> tag can be set to play a specific number of times, or continuously whilst the page containing the sounds remains displayed.

However, to cover most browsers, usually, the HTML <EMBED> tag is a better choice as it is supported in most current browsers including Netscape v2.0 and later versions.

See your HTML guide or Web design software documentation for more precise information.

RealAudio: live audio streaming

In a Web page containing a discrete sound clip, the sound file has to fully download to a visitor's browser before it can play. With live audio streaming, however, sound can be played and heard while downloading to a visitor's Web browser.

You can discover more about RealAudio technology at Progressive Networks' website. Point your browser at: www.realaudio.com/.

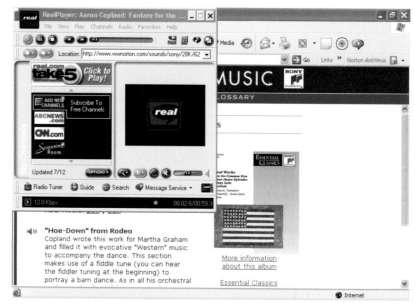

RealAudio from Progressive Networks is currently one of the most popular live audio streaming systems on the Internet. A visitor's browser must support live audio streaming – some older browsers may not (thankfully, most people now have compatible browsers).

Also, your Web host must support the variety of RealAudio technology you want to use, so liaise closely with them to determine the options available to you.

Many radio stations worldwide now use RealAudio technology to deliver their programs to the world through the Web.

Creating RealAudio content

You'll need to download and install the following (currently free) software: 1. PresenterOne and 2. GRiNS Editor for RealOne Player. Also try: http://www.realnetworks.com/developers/index.html. Next, you can learn how to create RealAudio using the superb guides available from real.com. Try: http://service.real.com/help/library/guides/production/realpgd.htm.

To provide a RealAudio-based news service, simply follow the guidelines listed in the RealAudio section earlier in this chapter.

For Web-based news sites to succeed, the content has to be compelling, relevant and interesting enough for visitors to want to return again and again to the site. You can add free newsfeeds to your site from www.moreover.com/.

Delivering a news service

News providers often broadcast directly onto the Web using RealAudio technology, and some also provide a text-based equivalent for those visitors who want to keep their viewing more private. Providing a Web news service also requires maintenance and upkeep. News, by its nature, happens erratically and continuously and events can change fast, creating huge logistical problems for site providers. Nevertheless, the benefits are seductive. Consider the following four examples:

- Organizations can include speeches and interviews made by key industry movers and shakers.

- Travel-oriented websites could include news about travel conditions in key parts of the world.

- Websites covering sports events like the round-the-world yacht races could include up-to-date news reports about the latest developments.

- Fashion-based Web pages could include talks from famous designers and models about the latest trends to hit their industry. And so on.

Web audio top tips

1   Consider carefully whether you really need audio. Sound demands more from a visitor's PC, requires sound hardware, and maybe a special plug-in at the browser end.

2   If you decide to include a sound component in your website, consider carefully whether you should set this to autoplay as soon as a visitor arrives at your page. Some visitors may become irritated with your choice of music or type of voice.

3   For a site containing autoplay music, ideally, include a Stop/Mute button and let your visitors choose whether to mute or listen to your sound clip.

4   Currently, the <BGSOUND> tag works only in those browsers that support it, like Internet Explorer, but not Netscape browsers. Netscape browsers make extensive use of plug-ins to handle a range of different file types.

5   Avoid using sound content to duplicate what is already included in your text. Provide essential information in text form and let audio content complement your presentation. Consider including a brief text description/overview of each audio component included.

6   Try to avoid including single sentence sound extracts: visitors may expect more and so become puzzled or irritated.

7   The simpler conventional sound formats .wav and .mid are ideal for sound clips of up to about 1 minute's duration. Any longer than this and visitors may become impatient.

8   Audioconferencing technology can also provide an ideal environment in which to informally discuss a range of issues, following in the Internet café and virtual clubs tradition.

Animating your Web pages

Movement, animation, sound and video components can all provide impact and grab the attention of your visitors. But success here needs careful consideration and handling. This chapter explores what is possible.

Covers

Chapter Ten

Introducing Web animation

Gaining animation skills

To apply complex animation-type components to your Web pages successfully requires some extra knowledge and skills using a variety of multimedia-type authoring programs, some of which may be expensive. As with any complex software, the process takes time and effort.

Under the guidance of a skilled graphic designer, incredibly effective results can be achieved with tools from Macromedia (for example). However, expensive and powerful software cannot make up for poor design choices, so taking the time and effort to learn about basic design techniques is always a worthwhile investment.

There's nothing stopping anyone from obtaining the necessary tools and learning these skills. Just allow for the extra time you think you'll need, double it, then add a bit more!

If your Web project is particularly urgent, often a more cost-effective strategy is simply to "buy in" the necessary skills from appropriate contract programmers and graphic artists rather than have to repeat the exercise several times later. Remember, these specialists have been over this same fence many times before, so usually can complete the job quicker.

Understanding more about your visitors

Visitors can be seen to fall into 2 categories (or a little of both).

Viewers

Viewers don't necessarily like to read a lot of information onscreen; they may prefer visual impact. They seek a seductive experience and the journey – not the destination. A tantalizing wash of color, fun and variety wrapped up in a few emotive words and phrases. Viewers usually love animation in all its forms.

Readers

Readers however, are different. They have a clear goal and are seeking something specific in your website. Often, they may turn off graphics capabilities in their browsers to speed up access to the information they want. To design your site for readers, pack your presentation with lots of relevant information and make the pages load fast over almost any browser and Web connection. Then provide easy to use, alternative ways to access the information.

Applying flashing components

To attract a visitor's attention quickly, a flashing object certainly gets noticed. However, a flashing component can also draw a visitor's attention away from the main message and too many conflicting elements can easily cause visitor confusion. Consider:

- Anything flashing on a Web page exerts a powerful pull.

- Including multiple flashing objects on a Web page can create a special blend of chaos, or provide stimulating excitement: the key point here is determining what's appropriate.

Flashing logos

A logo is usually the central branding component. Therefore, consider carefully before causing a logo to flash. Nevertheless, a flashing logo in a lighter context may work well as part of the whole presentation.

Flashing text

Paragraphs are usually best left as plain text: a visitor needs time to focus on your message. Anything that interferes with this essential process doesn't usually help.

Here's a quick way to steal a visitor's attention: provide a single headline or short sentence, suggest impact or urgency, then make it blink. Like a lighthouse beacon, flashing text exerts a powerful pull on the eye. Likewise, a flashing frame tends to draw the eye towards the frame contents. If this is what you're aiming for, fine.

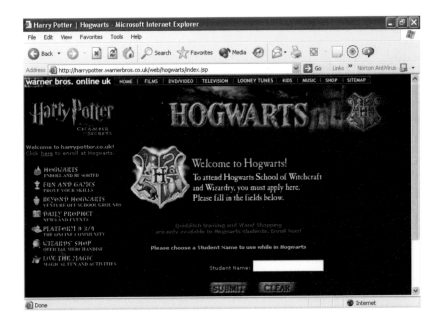

Using animated GIFs

Animated Web pages demand more from a browser than their static counterparts. For example, using too many dynamic GIFs with infinite loops can use up an excessive amount of a visitor's computer resources and so create temporary operating system instability.

Static Web pages don't include any movement or animation, only text and ideally some graphics content. Dynamic Web pages include components which provide action or movement of some kind. Although the idea of dynamic Web pages may at first seem more appealing, it's possible for this aspect to be overdone.

Sometimes, a static Web page can be adequate for your needs and it can put over the desired impression simply and effectively. However, if you feel your Web page is missing that "extra something", one answer might be to "spice up" the page by adding an animated or dynamic GIF.

What is a dynamic GIF?

A dynamic GIF is simply several slightly different GIF images linked together to form a chain almost like a film sequence. For example, there may be ten or fifteen frames in such a sequence.

Ideally, a dynamic GIF should be carefully designed to produce a small physical size. However, remember that a poorly designed and badly prepared dynamic GIF is arguably worse than using a single still image.

A dynamic GIF can be set up to:

Be careful not to provide too much movement on a page to avoid creating a condition whereby a visitor's eye is continually attracted to various, sometimes opposing, elements, thus creating confusion. A visitor can then miss any central message entirely.

- Run through its sequence once when a visitor logs on to a Web page.

- Loop through a sequence a set number of times. The interval between each frame can also be specified.

- Loop indefinitely (see the BEWARE tip).

Creating a dynamic GIF

A wide range of applications are now available to help you create dynamic or animated GIFs. You can use standalone programs like Animation Shop from Paint Shop Pro, and software like GIF Animator from Alchemy Mindworks at: www.mindworkshop. com/alchemy/alchemy.html.

Or you can learn to use the animation tools that may come built-in as part of the top quality Web design software products.

Microsoft's ActiveX

In some ways a complement to Java, Microsoft's ActiveX enables a specific applet to be designed to perform a specific task.

ActiveX applications include: multimedia animation; virtual reality; calendars; animated buttons; Web forms; viewing Microsoft Office files in Internet Explorer; video sequences; and other types of dynamic Web content. You can create your own ActiveX controls, or you can find many already available on the Web (see the tips).

If a browser needs an ActiveX control that is not present, usually a visitor is prompted to download the control automatically from an appropriate Web provider.

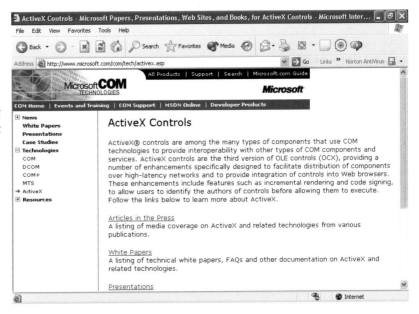

Shockwave (page 99) was one of the first ActiveX controls to be included with Microsoft's Internet Explorer and Windows 9x. Other ActiveX controls include RealAudio (Chapter 9).

To discover more about ActiveX, point your browser at: http://www.activex.com and search the Web.

ActiveX components run on any PC that has an ActiveX-compliant Web browser installed – for example, Microsoft's Internet Explorer v3.0 and later.

Including ActiveX components in your Web pages

To place an ActiveX component in your Web page, you can use the HTML <OBJECT> tag, or better still, use the appropriate commands in your Web design software. See your documentation for the exact syntax you need and try working with ActiveX.

Java and Java beans

Working with Java (from Sun Microsystems)

Java is a programming language that you can use to create multimedia Web components. A Java applet is a small type of Java program that can be placed on a HTML Web page.

Java applets usually work best on Pentium-grade computers to benefit fully from the special effects they provide. As most PCs today are Pentium-driven, the risk of problems is much lessened.

Examples include sophisticated animation sequences, often including sound and video clips and the now familiar ticker-tape streamers that provide up-to-date relevant news often visible on many Web pages. Java applets are also platform-independent so can run on Microsoft Windows, Apple Macs and UNIX operating systems without any need for further editing or modification.

Java demands more of a PC's resources and slows down page loading. The viewing browser must also support Java. More rarely nowadays, some PCs may not be able to handle Java properly, possibly leading to confusion and poor presentation on those PCs.

Providing Java applets in your Web pages

A Java applet must download to a visitor's PC completely before it can run. Contrast this trait with JavaScript on the following page.

Consider the following guidelines:

- You can learn to write your own applets. Java is a continually developing language.

- Lots of different applets have already been developed (see the HOT TIP). Simply modify these to work correctly.

To place a Java applet on a Web page, use the <APPLET> tag and its attributes as described in your HTML guide or Web design software. You'll need .class files and several other types of files to install an applet.

Using Java beans in a Web page

There are lots of sites on the Web from which you can download free Java applets. Use search engines and directories to find the ones you want to use.

A Java bean is a Java applet designed to be one component in a larger application; unlike a Java applet which requires several type of files, a Java bean contains all you need to install the applet.

Example beans are sometimes provided with Web design applications that support them. For example, NetObjects Fusion v4.0 includes an example bean that calculates the current date and time in several geographical locations.

JavaScript and JScript

Developed by Netscape, JavaScript is a type of programming language loosely related to Java; JavaScript is considered to be less complex and so easier to learn. However, like Java, JavaScript has the potential to cause security problems – sometimes linked to computer viruses.

A JavaScript component can run as soon as a Web page loads or can be activated by a visitor clicking on a button or contacting some other trigger point on a Web page.

Cookies are tiny code modules that let you store some brief basic information on a visitor's PC for use later when the visitor revisits the relevant cookie-driven website.

JavaScript is often used to place cookies (see the DON'T FORGET tip) in a Web page, to help record key information such as a visitor's browser, plug-ins, operating system and display monitor resolution. When a visitor next logs on to a website, a cookie can help identify that visitor so that a personalized "Welcome back *[person's name]*" message is displayed.

Including JavaScript in a Web page

As with Java, you can learn JavaScript and write your own JavaScript components. Alternatively, you can download predesigned components and modify these to work with your Web pages. Whichever option you choose, it's useful to learn at least the basics of JavaScript (see "JavaScript in easy steps" for more details).

A JavaScript applet does not have to be downloaded fully to work, and is therefore usually faster than pure Java.

You can insert JavaScript using the <SCRIPT> tag in HTML or by arranging for the JavaScript code to run when a specified event occurs. See your Web design software, HTML and JavaScript guides for detailed design options.

JScript

JScript represents Microsoft's alternative to JavaScript. Whereas JavaScript was developed with Netscape Navigator in mind, JScript is tightly integrated with the Microsoft Internet Explorer series of Web browsers. Unfortunately, this often means that a component developed for JScript may not work under JavaScript.

Within the public mainstream, JavaScript has really taken precedence over JScript nowadays, but the latter may still yet re-emerge as a formidable force. Only time will tell. For now, the best advice is to simply stay with JavaScript as this approach is compatible with most modern Web browsers and looks set to stand the test of time.

Example JavaScript: detecting a visitor's browser

Here's an example of how JavaScript can be used to detect whether a visitor is using Microsoft Internet Explorer 4.x or later.

If yes, our visitor is redirected to an alternative Index page on the website server that contains the imaginary site: "Yourcompany" which includes more powerful DHTML animated effects. The script below could be placed between the <HEAD> and </HEAD> tags in the default Home/Index page:

Throughout this book, we have included some JavaScript examples. If you use these examples, make sure you type every single character correctly, and where you see quotes, use straight quotes like this ("), not curly quotes like this ("). Ideally, first spend some time learning the basics of JavaScript.

```
<SCRIPT>
<!—
if ((navigator.userAgent.indexOf("MSIE")!=-1) && navigator.app
Version.substring(0,1) > 3)
{
window.location.replace("http://www.Yourcompany.com/
index_mie4.html");
}
//—>
</SCRIPT>
```

Modify the script above, substituting the Web address and Index page name that you want to use. Other free scripts are available.

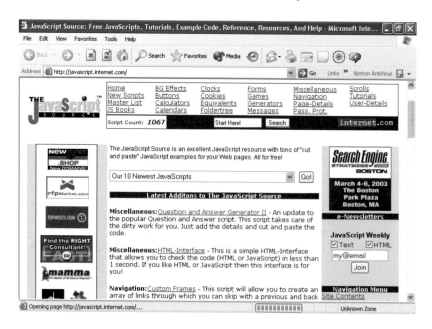

Using rollover buttons and pictures

The term rollover is used to describe a picture, icon or button that changes when the mouse pointer is moved over it, and which may also optionally change another related image at the same time too.

Rollovers won't work with imagemap-type graphics. Imagemaps have hotspots defined as hyperlinks instead.

Other names that refer to rollovers include: mouseover, hover and animated (buttons). The currently popular rollover technique usually involves using some JavaScript code and provides another useful tool in the Web designer's toolkit. As a result, rollovers are simple to write, use little code and so therefore run quickly in a visitor's Web browser.

Because rollovers are seductive and appealing, it's easy to fall into the trap of providing rollover components that do little to add to the value of a page. Yet, with careful design, rollovers can provide an attractive, effective part of an overall Web page design.

How rollovers work

A basic rollover image is actually two images: one image that forms the default or "Off" condition and another to create the "On" or rollover condition. For the entire rollover to be seamless, both images must be precisely the same size and shape. As the images must display quickly, often small GIF image formats are used (see Chapter 7 for more information about images).

Here's one popular application for a rollover button you might want to consider when designing your own pages. In this example, when a visitor moves their mouse pointer onto one of the buttons on the right, the rollover on the left displays more details about that particular section.

Popular uses for rollovers

Rollovers can be particularly effective when used to create a series of site navigation buttons.

Because a tiny percentage of browsers still don't support JavaScript, visitors using these may not be able to see any rollovers you create. In practice, however, browsers are mostly free, and the vast majority of users already have JavaScript-compatible versions. Therefore, possible compatibility problems may not even be an issue. You decide.

For example, a green hyperlinked Web navigation button with white or light-colored text could, when the mouse pointer is placed on it, change to, say, a light beige color overlaid with black text. Move the mouse pointer away and the original dark green background color returns. In the example, the current active page is shown in orange with white text, ensuring all navigation states are displayed clearly .

Or, imagine you have a Web shop. For each product, you display a small thumbnail image. You can design a rollover so that when a visitor places their mouse pointer onto the image, the product picture is replaced with its current price, until our imaginary visitor moves the mouse pointer away to reveal the original thumbnail.

This approach allows pieces of crucial information to occupy the same physical space and provides the price only to those visitors who want that information, contributing to a more "clean" design structure and enabling more empty (but active) space to be utilized.

Creating a rollover

Many of the current Web design and graphics software packages like NetObjects Fusion, Microsoft FrontPage and Macromedia Fireworks provide commands to create rollovers.

When preparing images for use in rollovers, make sure that none of your GIF images are transparent. A transparent image will show the other image that makes up the rollover pair.

However, below is a basic example rollover HTML code:

```
<A HREF="rollover12.html"
onMouseover="document.but.src='images/button12_on.gif';"
onMouseout="document.but.src='images/button12_off.gif';">
<IMG SRC="images/button12_off.gif" NAME="but" ALT="[Product/
Price rollover button]"></A>
```

Whatever label you use in "NAME=... " above (we've used the label "but" in our example) remember: you must also place the label between "document" and "src" exactly as shown above.

Animating text on a Web page

Grabbing attention with JavaScript text boxes

JavaScript can be used to create a small text box window containing cycling testimonials. Imagine the selling power of 7 or 8 brief cycling testimonials each with, say, an onscreen display time of about 3–5 seconds. For businesses especially, real, verifiable, believable testimonials have immense influence.

You can create text boxes like this using simple JavaScript commands. Or with NetObjects Fusion, you can purchase "Components" from companies like http://club.coolmaps.com/. Using the Coolmaps' "RoboText" Component, you don't need to know JavaScript, just follow the simple instructions provided.

Animating the browser status bar

Also with JavaScript, you can arrange for a visitor's browser status bar to show scrolling messages. An excellent way to include up-to-the-minute information or details of special offers, etc.

The downside is that this effect can usually cause a Web page to load more slowly in your visitor's browser. If your page loads quickly, this may not be a problem; however, it's best avoided for graphically-rich Web pages.

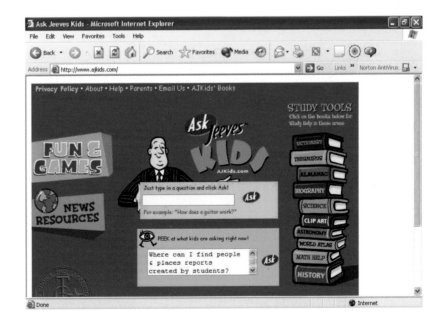

Adding a ticker-tape streamer

An ideal way to quickly help focus a visitor's attention is to provide a line of text scrolling across the screen; this "scrolling marquee" is much like a ticker-tape streamer. Ticker-tape banners can provide an eye-catching headline to communicate something important, announce a special promotion or to evoke tension. There are several ways you can do this in a Web page, for example, using:

- the HTML <MARQUEE></MARQUEE> tag-pair.

- Java language techniques.

- JavaScript.

Note: currently, the HTML <MARQUEE> tag is supported by Internet Explorer but not usually Netscape browsers. Browsers that support this feature will then scroll text across the screen as defined by the HTML/Java/JavaScript parameters.

Creating ticker tape streamers is easy with modern design software like FrontPage, Dreamweaver and NetObjects Fusion. Using the TickerTape2 Component from http://club.coolmaps.com for NetObjects Fusion, you can also specify font, colors and the type of text movement you want.

Here's one ideal application for a ticker tape streamer. This site wants to draw particular attention to its range of alternative payment options. So as soon as the Home page loads, the animated movement draws the eye in to the initial focus point: the ticker tape streamer (it looks considerably less effective in a static illustration!).

Captivating with Shockwave

A plug-in is a mini program attached to your browser which lets it handle unusual file formats.

Using Macromedia Shockwave, you can create high quality multimedia, animated graphics and sound components that display relatively quickly by using efficient compression technology. Shockwave is powerful: text, graphics, animation, video and sound sequences can all be combined easily. See: www.shockwave.com.

For a browser to read Shockwave, it must have the appropriate Shockwave plug-in installed and set up. The latest versions of Netscape Navigator/Communicator and Microsoft's Internet Explorer are, by default, already set up to handle basic Shockwave files.

Shockwave animations usually work best when supporting the main theme made up of simple text and graphics. Web pages containing Shockwave and ActiveX content demand more resources from a PC than those containing more traditional Web page elements. Fortunately, many visitors now have modern PCs that can easily cope with Shockwave demands.

As Shockwave is bitmap-based, components take longer to download compared to newer vector technologies like Flash (see overleaf). Shockwave files use the .dir and .dcr file formats and come in several varieties that are usually updated regularly.

You can include Shockwave technology on a Web page using the <EMBED> HTML tag. The best Web design software provides easy-to-use commands to place your ActiveX components on the page. See your Web design software guide for more details.

Captivating with Flash

Today, Flash essentially sets the standard if you want to create a high quality interactive and animated Web display. Flash enables a designer to create Flash "movies" that are scalable and use vector technology (rather than bitmap), so can provide great detail.

For more information about Flash technology, see: www. macromedia.com/ software/flash/.

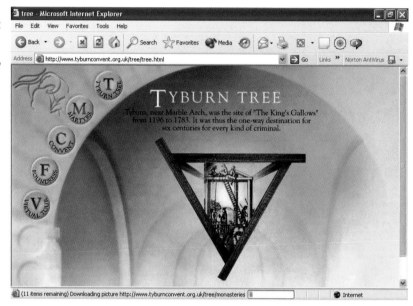

If you plan to include animated components in your Web pages, the search engines are ideal tools to help you find out as much as possible about the subject you want.

Also, this means Flash files (.swf format) are comparatively small, usually download more quickly than the earlier Shockwave technology and provide fast playback on typical modem-based connections. To "play" Flash animations, the Flash Player is required at the browser end. Fortunately, the Flash Player is now provided as part of the Windows and Apple Mac operating systems.

Typically, a Flash file uses an area called "the stage" to arrange several "frames" that make up the film sequence. Skilled Flash creators can build interesting, attractive and engaging scenes.

Using a later version of Flash you can even arrange for a static image to be seen for those browsers that don't have the Flash Player installed! Typical uses include Web advert banners and unique user interfaces. If a Flash animation does not appear to work properly, ask your Web host to check that they have the correct MIMIE types installed for Flash.

Introducing Web video technology

Web video enables film, TV and news clips to be made available through a Web page in two different ways:

- A discrete video clip file that must be fully downloaded before it can be viewed (early systems).

- A live video streaming clip which can be viewed as it is downloading (the latest technology):

Benefits

- Video is humanizing: it can put over warmth, personality, emotion, feelings, tension and passion.

- International visitors may understand spoken language better than text displayed on your Web pages.

- Moving pictures can describe complexities effectively.

- Video is undoubtedly a powerful advertising medium!

Drawbacks

- Web video can make heavy demands on a visitor's PC.

- The technology is still a relatively new and complex development requiring more complex tools.

- Spoken language may be difficult to understand sometimes.

Evaluating whether Web video is for you

Consider the following guidelines:

1. Read all of the pages relating to the use of video in this chapter. Use the Web to find out more information.

2. Few visitors will wait more than 3 or 4 minutes maximum for a file to download, unless the benefit for waiting is clear. Try to keep files sizes small to minimize downloading time.

3. For visitors with slower modem connections, downloading video files may be impractical. Assess your visitors' needs.

4. To put over a mood of fast action, changing scenes or subtle movement, video may be ideal. If you want to encourage pause and consideration, it's usually best to stick with carefully crafted text and graphics content.

5. Always remember: ill-considered use of video can overshadow the central message, usually best left as text.

For more information about QuickTime from Apple, point your browser at: www. apple.com/quicktime/.

If the video sequence you want to use is brief, consider using Shockwave or Flash instead. Why? File sizes are smaller than conventional video and so usually download quicker, providing a more efficient delivery. However, remember: to create a lasting impression, video sometimes has its own special kind of irreplaceable impact.

Popular Web video technologies

Microsoft AVI file format (.avi)

AVI (Audio Video Interleaved) remains one of the most popular multimedia formats for adding discrete movie content to a website.

QuickTime Multimedia (.mov, .qt)

If movement is an important feature of your website, a video sequence can arguably illustrate what you want to put over better than any other type of content.

QuickTime is a popular multimedia software system from Apple. In a QuickTime "movie", you can include graphics, text, music, video, sound and 3D components. However, for visitors to view a QuickTime clip in your Web page, they must have the correct plug-in installed for their browser and operating system.

MPEG movies (.mpg, .mpeg, .mpe, .mpv)

Web browser plug-ins necessary to view MPEG files are available for Microsoft Windows and the Apple Macintosh.

The Vivo Active Producer format (.viv)

The Vivo multimedia format is supported by Microsoft Windows and the Apple Mac and also requires an appropriate browser plug-in/player to view the movie files. Not so common nowadays.

A fast ISDN or ADSL (Broadband) Internet connection provides an ideal environment in which to view RealVideo files. As the cost of a Broadband Internet connection is falling fast, more and more people are now enjoying viewing video clips without the often stop-start jerky action of slower, modem-based connections.

RealMedia (.rm, .ra) and RealPlayer Media (.rpm)

With live video streaming, visitors can play and view a video clip *while* it's downloading so they do not have to download a large file just to identify what it's about. One of the most popular live video streaming technologies is RealVideo from Progressive Networks. RealVideo offers the following significant advantages over previous delivery systems:

- RealVideo player software installed on a visitor's PC can sense when there's heavy Internet traffic and compensate to minimize problems. RealVideo aims to provide the most stable picture quality possible under varying conditions.

- Additional controls like Fast Forward, Rewind and Search are easier to integrate with RealVideo streaming technology.

- RealVideo also includes advanced error correction.

Including video on a Web page

A video component can be embedded into a Web page or linked to it. An embedded video clip is usually downloaded automatically when a visitor logs on to the Web page.

A linked component usually includes control buttons to enable visitors to decide if they want to play the sequence. To include a video in a Web page, perform the following:

1   You can provide a video sequence using the HTML sequence:

    <A HREF= "1video.rm">Click here to see the video</A>

    Ensure the video file has the correct filename extension for the type of video file. Or, you may be able to use the <EMBED> tag in your HTML document. See your HTML guide for more details.

Some of the latest browsers come with video players built in. For example. Netscape includes LiveVideo. Yet key video players can be included as part of a computer's operating system too, or are already freely available. If relevant, consider including a link to the source site so visitors can easily gain access to the appropriate plug-in should they need it.

2   (Optional) With modern Web page design software, the task is usually made much easier than in Step 1. See the appropriate documentation for precise instructions.

3   (Optional) Include any other HTML attributes – for example, video playing position, the number of times the video sequence plays and the size of the playing window.

4   Test before going live.

Once visitors click on the link on your Web page representing the RealVideo file, their operating system opens their installed RealVideo player and starts to play the video sequence.

The playback sequence may be interrupted if significant Internet congestion is present. Buttons may be made available offering fast forward, rewind and search.

Animation: top hints and tips

Having powerful animation technologies at your fingertips is a great temptation. Animation can help transform a website into a memorable "exciting experience". The key to success here, though, is making the right choices: in other words, deciding what's appropriate and what isn't.

Animation is ideal when trying to put over a mass of detailed information. Information can be structured into digestible blocks, each of which need only be made visible in sequence, at the correct time, and by the movement of a visitor's mouse.

1 If a page contains some animation sequences, tell your visitors so they won't be puzzled by gaps if they're viewing with animations turned off.

2 Often, successful animation advertising works best if you provide further compelling reasons for a visitor to stay. Perhaps use a simple interactive game or quiz to provide an incentive for a visitor to stay online and bookmark the site.

3 When covering the topic of movement, development or changing states, animation can be particularly beneficial. For example, when showing key stages in a cooking recipe; or in illustrating the biological growth of an organism; or simply to show the development cycle of a product.

Navigating a complex website can be made easier through animation. For example, a cheerful cartoon character could move around the screen indicating links to places of interest.

4 If the subject matter can be interpreted as boring or lacking excitement, sometimes applying creative animation techniques can spruce up a Web page and heighten interest.

5 Animation does not have to be "loud" to be effective. Small elements like sparkles or comet-type effects can sometimes make a greater impact.

6 For website topics involving abstract ideas and concepts or which may be difficult to visualize, animation techniques can offer a welcome boost.

7 Consider carefully the use of animated games and humor on a site which deals with sensitive issues.

Key hints on what not to animate

There's no simple answer about what not to animate. Learn much about your target visitor. This knowledge helps define how to approach the design task. Only you, the Web page designer, really know what is best for your site and for your visitors – although often this is a learning experience. Consider the following points:

- Keep the Home/Index page "pure". Large animated elements create additional download time, so may not be appreciated by visitors who may be unsure that your site is relevant.

- Don't animate a page simply because you know how to "work Flash" and enjoy creating animations! Let the purpose of your page dictate its content.

- Visitors who are essentially seeking information, yet who become distracted by inappropriate animated elements, may become so irritated that they leave – gone in a click! Enticing a visitor to return after a "bad" experience is much harder than trying to win over a new visitor.

- If the central important message of a Web page is text-or graphic-based, including animated elements will probably not help but only confuse the issue.

This organization on the right has chosen a simple, clean, uncluttered style. The blue underline for links has been removed providing a clearer view. Additionally, stylish shadow-type rollover buttons provide a touch of uniqueness.

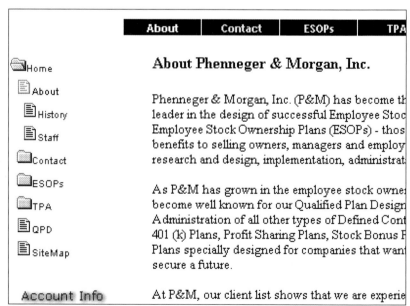

Building in the power components

This chapter explores some of the options open to you to make your website more interactive, helpful and useful to visitors. You'll also learn how you can password-protect a website or limit access to specific pages.

Covers

Chapter Eleven

Adding a drop-down "Go" menu

A drop-down menu is an ideal way to provide multiple choice or multiple navigation options within a small physical space.

A drop-down menu can be activated simply by making a choice or by making a choice plus clicking a "Go" button.

Most of the worthwhile WYSIWYG Web design software like Dreamweaver, FrontPage and NetObjects Fusion help make the job of creating a drop-down menu easy.

You can discover hundreds of scripts available from Matt's script archives at: www.scriptarchive.com/ or http://javascript.internet.com/

For NetObjects Fusion users, a Go-menu component comes with the package. Or you can purchase the more powerful "LinkMaster" – a JavaScript-based add-on component – from http://club. coolmaps.com. This means that creating a drop-down Go-type menu that works first time is simple. And you don't need to know JavaScript: just follow the simple and clear instructions.

If you're not using NetObjects Fusion, or you're feeling more adventurous, you can create a "Go" drop-down menu using your own JavaScript or a CGI script.

Including a website Search box

For a growing website, one of the most useful tools you can provide is an easy website search tool. You can do this using a special CGI script or through using JavaScript code.

Many free sources exist on the Net from which you can download the code and adapt it for your website (get permission first).

This site has chosen to place a Search box in a highly prominent location on the Home/Index page.

Some Web design software may include predesigned "components" or routines that can make the job of creating a website Search facility much easier.

For example: the SiteSearch component from http://club. coolmaps.com for NetObjects Fusion provides an easy-to-install JavaScript-based search tool that runs on the Web browser.

Creating a Sitemap page

The more pages that make up a website, the harder and more confusing site navigation may become for your visitors. You can make site navigation on larger sites easier by providing an up-to-date Sitemap or Table of Contents page.

Some of the better Web design software tools may also include predesigned "components" for easy creation and ongoing maintenance of a Sitemap page or website Table of Contents.

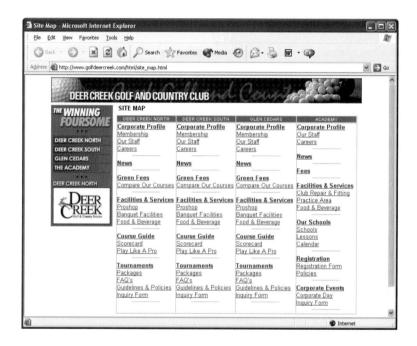

Microsoft FrontPage includes a superb Table of Contents "FrontPage component" that can easily create titles and text links for every page in a website.

Or, the "SiteMap" component from http://club.coolmaps.com for NetObjects Fusion also provides an easy-to-install JavaScript-based Sitemap tool that loads quickly and runs on the visitor's Web browser.

Furthermore, Coolmaps also have a smart DHTML-based "SiteIndex" component that displays a popup scrolling window that contains all the pages in the site. A visitor can then quickly and easily click the desired page name, to move to the page they want.

Prompting with a popup box

To provide a special type of interactivity to a website, you can add a popup box that "pops up" overlaid on the existing browser window when a visitor clicks a specific link, visits a particular page, or runs their mouse over an object. For example, you could arrange for a "Welcome" popup box to display. A visitor could then read the brief marketing message or details of a special promotion, then click the OK button to cause the main Home/Index page to appear.

However, use popup boxes with consideration: they can irritate visitors if too many popup instances occur. Ask yourself whether your choice really adds value. Both Dreamweaver and NetObjects Fusion help make the task of creating popup boxes much easier.

Visitors can become irritated if the same popup box keeps appearing while they navigate a site. Therefore, here's an idea: limit the number of times a popup box appears to no more than 2.

If you're using a website entry popup box, don't force regular visitors to view this box each time they log on: you can use cookies that automatically allow repeat visitors to bypass the box. Precise popup control can be done easily with Steve Shaw's wonderful PopupMaster Pro at: www.popupmaster.com.

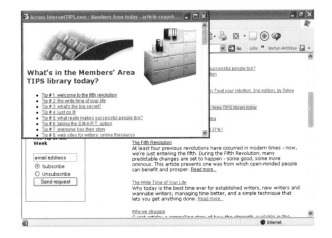

1   For a JavaScript-based popup, you'll need to include the JavaScript script between the <HEAD> and </HEAD> tags in the page from which the popup box originates.

2   Enter the desired height and width settings in the Script to ensure the popup box is the size and shape you want.

3   Next, create your popup page containing the information that you want to put in the popup box.

4   Save your changes. Start your Web browser and test the popup. You may need to tweak the settings and repeat these steps a few times to ensure your popup performs the way you want.

Plug-ins, viewers and helpers

A bewildering range of file types exists designed to work with special file formats, like those from Microsoft Word, PowerPoint, Excel and perhaps ODBC database files.

To find out more about using Adobe Acrobat files, an ideal starting place to visit is: www.adobe.com/

To ensure their files are available to as many people as possible, many providers have created plug-ins, file viewers and helper applications that work with a Web browser to allow certain files to be made available on the Web.

Plug-ins are available for a wide range of file types. These include Real.com's RealPlayer G2; Macromedia's Shockwave and Flash; Adobe Acrobat files; Apple's QuickTime; RealSpace FlashPix; Headspace Beatnik files; and Cosmo (a virtual reality tool), to name but a few.

Maintaining a true reproduction of the original

Imagine you want to make available on your website (exactly as it appears in print) a company brochure or desktop published story.

If the choice of font and exact layout is particularly important, one option is to convert your brochure or other document to Adobe's Acrobat Portable Document Format (.PDF).

Plug-ins are available for different platforms. Make sure your visitors understand that they'll need the correct browser plug-in for the particular operating system they're using.

PDF includes all the essential information to create an electronic representation of an original document, following the same layout and choice of fonts. PDF files are compact, portable and can be viewed on a wide range of different platforms.

Not surprisingly, then, PDF is now one of the most popular document formats available on the Net, and looks set to be the universal document type of the future. Time will tell.

How plug-ins work at the browser end

Using your chosen Web design software, you insert a special document into a Web page; this is identified as a small picture or icon after you've published your Web page to the Web.

To view the special document, visitors then click the icon to have the file download to their PC or appear in their browser. However, for this to happen they must have the correct plug-in for their browser and operating system.

Dealing with unusual file formats

Firstly, if possible, try to avoid providing information in an unusual format: often, these types of files can be converted to more "standard" formats, like PDF. However, if that is not an option for you, consider the steps below:

1. Learn about the particular plug-in you want to use. Often, the best way of doing this is to point your browser at the Home page of the specific plug-in provider. Here you can glean a lot of useful information and possibly advice.

2. Insert the plug-in content onto your desired Web page using the <EMBED> tag and its attributes in HTML. See your HTML guide for details on the exact syntax to use.

3. Mention the name of the unusual format used and optionally provide some brief background information on your Web page, so visitors can access more information.

If you include these links to plug-in providers, ideally make the link open a second browser window so they will still have access to your site in the first browser window.

Why send visitors away from your site after you've spent much time and effort getting them to visit in the first place?

4. To provide the means whereby your visitors can view or use files stored in unusual formats, it's essential to provide a link to the website containing the plug-in application a visitor needs to view these unusual files.

5. Ensure the Web link address you provide in Step 4 is valid and up-to-date: test it regularly by downloading the file yourself and running the application.

6. Provide brief but clear instructions on what a visitor has to do to view or to use any unusual files or documents provided on your Web pages.

How www.grc.com provide PDF access:

The SpinRite 5.0 Brochure   4 pages

This four page brochure provides a quick overview of SpinRite 5.0's major features, benefits, and capabilities.

● Download this Adobe Acrobat file. (43 Kbytes)

Quick-and-easy JavaScript solutions

Lots of different JavaScript routines are already available on the Web. Many are free, but make sure you have permission to use them first, especially if you're creating a business website. For example, take a look at: http:// javascript.internet.com/.

All of the special effects or "components" listed on this page use third-party pre-built mini-applications, usually using JavaScript. But why reinvent the wheel? With components from http://club. coolmaps.com for NetObjects Fusion Web design software, you don't need to know JavaScript. What's more, they're reliable, easy to install, easy to use, and updated regularly to match the current browsers. Here's some information on just a few components:

Uploading and linking to files the easy way

The FileAway component lets you easily and quickly upload and link to various files. First, you simply install the component, then tell FileAway the types of files you're using and their folders/ directories. FileAway automatically provides links to these files on your page. The component then uploads these files to your website server (PC) located at your Web host's premises. That's it!

Control how popup windows behave

Both http://club. coolmaps.com and NetObjects Fusion provide excellent tutorials and problem-solving support from their websites.

See: www.coolmaps.com/ and www.websitepros.com respectively.

JavaScript popup windows can now be tamed with the RemoteControl component. You can also arrange for a "remote control" window to popup and stay on top of the main window! Great for advertising but can irritate users.

Display random images

Have your website update itself automatically. To arrange for a different image to appear each time a visitor loads a page, or have an image change after a specific time delay, you can use the RandomActs component.

Providing a Web slideshow

In a Web slideshow, you can arrange for an image to change when a visitor clicks on another button or location on the page. A visitor can then cycle forwards and backwards through a series of images. Great for showing the family holiday snaps or displaying a range of products! The SlideShow component from http://club.coolmaps.com does exactly that.

Change an image when a mouse glides over it

Give your website an instant style. The RollOver component can not only change its own image but also other selected images. It can change the "roll-off" delay time as well!

Inserting a dynamic calendar onto a Web page

Never forget another date! Using the Coolmaps.com BlindDate component, you can insert a basic calendar. You can choose dates up to 1 year in advance and link to special pages that can describe events due to occur on those dates.

For lots of PERL CGI scripts (many free) that you can use to enhance your pages, take a look at Matt's script archive at: www.scriptarchive.com/.

Place a date and time digital clock on a page

You can use the OClock component to quickly place a date and time clock anywhere on your page and set the time to your own time zone. Visitors see the current time in your time zone. This component uses graphics not text to create the time display.

For lots more help in creating a website, whether you're just starting or a seasoned pro, consider visiting these two wonderful sites to find lots of useful information, hints and tips: www.devx.com/projectcool/ or www.boogiejack.com.

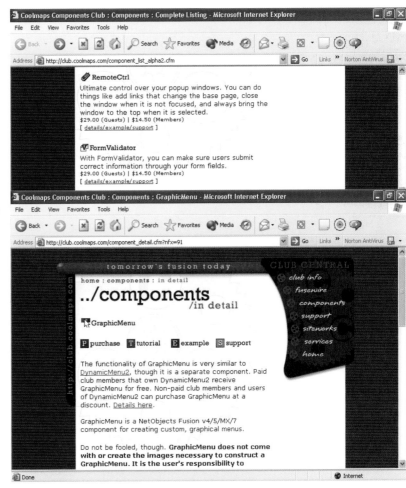

Password-protecting your website

If you provide pages containing sensitive, special, important or up-to-date information, you may want to provide access on a subscription basis, or give access to authorized persons only – like employees. Using password-based access systems, you can lock out a single page, a series of pages, an entire group of pages or even an entire website.

For low-security options, you can use a JavaScript option designed using off-the-shelf Web design software.

If you want to create a more powerful and self-running Members Only or subscription-based website, with a higher level of security than that provided using basic JavaScript, check out the Master Members Only CGI script from www.willmaster.com.

One simple low-security solution for NetObjects Fusion users

ProtectIT is a NetObjects Fusion component from http://club. coolmaps.com that provides a quick and simple solution to password-protecting specific pages on your website. Currently, you can create up to 20 passwords per page and, with a little imagination, you could create a system that ensures passwords are changed at regular or irregular intervals, to build a higher level of security. However, this is not a high-security system.

Website security in Microsoft FrontPage

In combination with the FrontPage Personal Web Server or the Microsoft Personal Web Server through the Administration commands, you can set up what FrontPage calls "Permissions" to allow Administrator, Author and Browsing access rights. See your FrontPage guide for details.

Security-critical options

For a high-security solution, you may need to have special encrypted files installed on your Web server. One solution is to use .htaccess on your Web host's servers to control access to specific files and therefore Web pages. Discuss options with your Web host.

Providing a discussion forum

What is a discussion forum

As communication-oriented species, our nature is to talk and discuss, so why not make use of that trait to benefit and enhance your website? But, there is a trade-off: the need for setup time and regular management and monitoring.

Creating a discussion forum can be one of the best ways to build an online community, meet new friends and forge new business associates. Many Web hosts provide a discussion forum as an optional part of a Web hosting package. Or, check out: www.network54.com/ and www.ultrascripts.com/.

A discussion forum, discussion group or bulletin board allows visitors to submit information, views, ideas and talents onto a regularly updated Web page for the benefit of all concerned. The "posts" can be viewed, commented on or replied to as necessary.

How to set up a discussion forum

Establishing a discussion forum is one of the best ways to encourage visitors to return. Visitors who contribute to your discussion forum are obviously interested in your field, so these people may represent hot prospects for your product or service.

Web design software from FrontPage and Fusion contains commands that enable you to set up discussion forums.

The best discussion forums ensure that you can closely monitor what is being said so that, if necessary, you can delete undesirable content and remove offenders from the list quickly.

However, liaise closely with your Web host or Internet Service Provider as you may need to use their CGI scripts or FrontPage Server Extensions, if appropriate.

Publishing your database

For some organizations, placing their entire database on the Web makes good commercial sense. For example, you might have thousands of product lines that you sell from your website with an inventory that changes daily: an ideal situation that probably demands an online database. However, this can be a particularly complex task, has clear security implications and should be considered carefully only after thorough investigation of the benefits, risks and drawbacks. Getting expert advice is a must.

Evaluating your options

Unless you're familiar with database design and have programming skills in a language such as PERL or mySQL, you'll need to spend many hours learning how to achieve each stage, or hire a competent programmer to do the work for you. Good database programmers, however, can be costly but essential if online databasing of your product line is the path you choose. Sometimes, you can save some money by doing some of the work in-house.

You can find many sources on the Net to help you learn more about database programming and decide the best solution for your particular needs. Plus, as software products become more user-friendly, working with Web databases is becoming easier!

1   You may not even need a full-blown database. Links 2.0 is a superb set of highly customizable scripts from which you can create a hierarchical structure. For more information, see: http://www.gossamer-threads.com/scripts/links/

NetObjects Fusion v4.x supports database production through Allaire ColdFusion or Microsoft ASP, without the need to write your own JScript or VBScript.

2   Otherwise, establish whether to host your website on a UNIX/Linux or a Windows NT server. Creating a database in NT is usually easier than using Linux, but is normally more costly. Also, NT is considered by some to be less robust.

3   Prefer the UNIX/Linux option? Choose PERL, ePERL or PHP scripts and commands to create your database.

4   If you choose NT, you could use Cold Fusion from Allaire to develop your database. Or you could opt for Microsoft Active Server Pages (ASP) using Java or Visual Basic. Whichever you choose, your server must be compatible with your choice or have the necessary "extensions" installed.

Gathering information with online forms

A Web form is a great information gatherer and all-round communications tool for both users and website providers. Here, you can learn the basics about Web forms and what you need to do to include various examples in your website.

Covers

Chapter Twelve

Why use Web forms?

A Web form is a powerful tool for any website and enables three important actions to take place on a Web page:

- Interactivity: a form allows direct interaction.

- Valuable user-related information can be gathered.

- Collected information can be processed and returned to the Web page provider, usually by automated email.

For business users Web forms can fulfil two essential necessities:

If you want to include forms in your Web pages, ask your ISP/Web host about the services and scripts they provide for processing forms. "Mailto", "formmail" and "SendMail" are three such popular scripts.

- Gathering the right kind of data. Accurate, key marketing-related global-oriented information is now so valuable, it has become a new kind of global currency.

- Receiving focused feedback about goods, services and website-related issues such as site useability, content relevancy and so on.

A carefully designed form can deliver focused results. To make full use of the data, you may need to process it elsewhere. With a carefully constructed form, this process can be made much easier.

The use of forms to process Web transactions is now also commonplace. Many of today's Web users already know they have some protection when buying online and so are more relaxed about leaving sensitive information like credit card details online while using secure servers.

See page 165.

How Web forms work

Web forms have two main components:

- The visible part: into which your visitors enter data.

- The invisible component: processes entered data and may store this information in a database for easy access; often achieved using a CGI script or Form handler script.

Once a visitor has completed entering their data into a Web form and clicked the Submit/Send button, this data is sent, stored and processed on the Web Forms server usually by carrying out the instructions in the CGI script as outlined in more detail below:

CGI scripts can carry out a range of other valuable tasks on a Web page. For example: fast-changing data such as stocks and shares can be displayed and updated on-the-fly. For more information, speak to your ISP, Web host or CGI-programmer.

Scripting options

Some Web hosts/ISPs support various kinds of Web form processing scripts. The Internet Service Provider Demon, for example, supports at least four basic types of script: forms processing, forms test script, page counter and "clickable" graphics. With some Web hosts/ISPs, you can pay for these extra services!

Scripts can be written in a variety of computer languages and are hosted on an ISP's servers; many ISPs offer script writing services. Ensure the script writer liaises closely with your Web host.

Basic form components

Web forms can be simple or complex in make-up. The more complex the design, the more finely-tuned can be your responses. Here are the most common Web form building blocks:

A Web page form need not have a plain look. If you have a series of Web pages based on a template, you may want to maintain continuity and perhaps include strong branding components or even advertisements. However, do consider the benefits and drawbacks of making a form too "busy", balanced against its central purpose of gaining information quickly and easily.

- Text entry boxes: allows space for a limited amount of text.

- Hidden fields: each character entered can be displayed as an asterisk (★) to hide sensitive information like passwords.

- Check boxes: to indicate one or more chosen options. A check box can be ticked (On) or cleared (Off).

- Radio buttons: allow only one of several options to be chosen. When a radio button is "On", all others in the related group are automatically turned "Off".

- Popup menus and scrolling menus: provide menu choices either as a fully displayed block or as multiple options made available through a scrollable list.

- Plain push-buttons: include two basic types. SUBMIT sends the form data to the server; RESET clears all form fields.

- Image push-buttons: an image icon instead of a gray box.

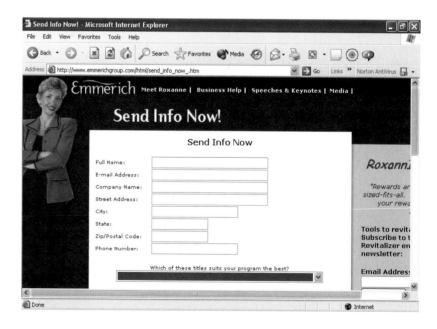

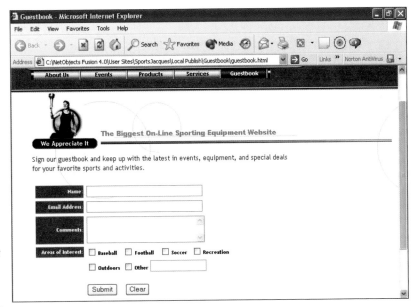

When you create a Web form in FrontPage, you can't test the form fully in Preview mode. When you publish your updated site to your FrontPage-compatible Web host, FrontPage creates a Submission page for the form. Testing should then be completed.

Using tables in Web forms

As you can see in the example above, table structures in a form are invaluable to help ensure that form components can be aligned vertically and horizontally, either with or without visible borders.

Often, a Web form includes a series of fields designed to prompt a visitor to enter details or make choices: name, address, email address, etc. Consider the following form design guidelines:

1 Without a table structure, each field directly below the field above may not be aligned vertically, so you can end up with a series of displaced fields which looks untidy.

2 Using a table structure, all these fields can be arranged in a column aligned neatly to one edge of the window.

3 Often, Web forms use a two-column table structure with as many rows as required. You can arrange for all the field titles to be placed in the left-hand column and the fields themselves in the right-hand column for perfect alignment, as shown above.

Creating an online form

You can create forms in one of two main ways:

- Build the components (text boxes, radio buttons, popup menu lists, etc.) one step at a time manually using any text editor or dedicated HTML editor. To create forms using this "hand coding" approach, you'll need to understand HTML sufficiently and have an eye for creating details accurately.

- Or use a graphical (WYSIWYG) Web design software package such as Microsoft FrontPage, Macromedia Dreamweaver, NetObjects Fusion or Adobe PageMill. These packages usually include several pre-built template forms that you can use "as is" or easily adapt to your needs.

Microsoft FrontPage forms use special FrontPage "components".
For these to work properly, your Web host must support them and have the correct FrontPage Server Extensions also installed.

Before getting started, consider the following guidelines:

1. Establish how you want to receive the form data. For information-gathering forms, you usually have several options, outlined in Steps 2, 3 and 4 below.

2. (Option) You can arrange for the form data to be copied to a text file and stored on your Web host's server.

3. (Option) Send the form data to an email address you specify.

For NetObjects Fusion users, http://club. coolmaps.com provide a forms solution. Their superb user friendly ClubMailer component and service allow you to send form results by email without any need to involve your Web host.

4. (Option) Use a CGI-script or Form Handler component stored on your Web host's server to perform further processing and actions on the information collected in your form and perhaps display a Confirmation/Thank you page to your visitor. Discuss options with your Web host as your forms and their servers must work together and "talk" the same language.

5. Most good Web hosts now provide a CGI-bin for their customers. A CGI-bin is essentially a storage location that may contain various standard scripts that can be used to process your forms. Common CGI scripts include formmail.pl and mailto.exe. If you use these services, ensure compatibility with your software.

Preventing bad input data

Sometimes a visitor may enter information incorrectly or enter irrelevant information into a field. For example, in a name field you wouldn't want a visitor to enter numbers. Remedy: ensure that the name field only accepts upper- and lower-case letters. Or when using date fields, you might want visitors to use a specific date format like dd/mm/yy or mm/dd/yyyy so you can easily import information into, say, a database program of some kind later.

Although form validation can be done with CGI on your Web server, JavaScript running on the visitor's PC usually performs the task much faster.

Sometimes, you might want to ensure that a visitor must enter information into specific fields in order to submit the form, or you might not want certain blank fields submitted. You just need to ensure that they provide all the information you ask, but try to make the process as quick and painless as possible to ensure a maximum sign-up or usage rate.

How to prevent bad input data

For lots of really useful (and often free) JavaScripts, one of the best sources on the Internet (in the author's opinion) is: http://javascript.internet.com/.

Usually, the simplest solution is to use a JavaScript routine. You can find many free snippets of code from generous providers on the Web (example: see the HOT TIP). Or if you use NetObjects Fusion, FormValidator is a great component from http://club. coolmaps.com that does exactly what we've discussed above.

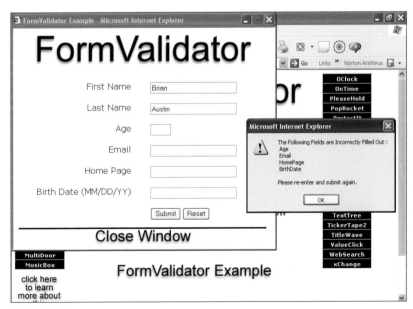

Installing a guestbook

Providing a guestbook form is a simple and effective option for many website owners. For those creating a personal website, a guestbook provides an easy way to get to know your visitors, meet new friends, and gain some feedback about your website.

For businesses, interaction and feedback with your visitors is essential. Any mechanism that you can add to your website to legally and morally capture an email address is money well spent (see the tip). When recording information about people, remember to check possible obligations with the Data Protection Registrar: www.open.gov.uk/dpr/dprhome.htm or other relevant body.

Creating a guestbook Web page

Although you can use raw HTML to build a guestbook page, many current Web design software packages provide pre-built guestbook templates that you can easily edit or adapt to suit your needs. FrontPage, NetObjects Fusion and HotMetal Pro include a range of form types including guestbook templates.

In fact, FrontPage also provides additional form templates: feedback, confirmation, user registration and even a form "Wizard" to help create unusual, unique and sometimes tricky form designs.

Visitors can receive thousands of irrelevant emails each year. This "email spam" wastes their valuable time and resources and so understandably can raise strong emotions. Protect your visitors' email address and include a Privacy statement/page demonstrating your commitment to maintaining their privacy.

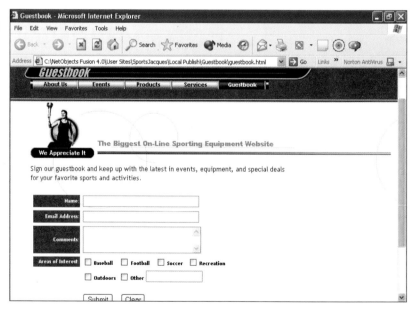

Providing a feedback/contact form

After putting in much time and creative effort designing a website, we can sometimes get distracted by concentrating too much on the details. However, what you may find easy, others may not, and vice versa. The key word here is "trust". You need to explore ways and options that quickly demonstrate that your website is not based on hype, but facts, value and authenticity.

One of the most beneficial things you can do to build a trusting relationship with your visitors is to ask them what they think about your website:

- Does the site meet their needs?

- Is the site easy to use?

- What more would they like to see?

- And so on.

Some statistics suggest that a visitor is twice as likely to fill in a feedback form than click on an email link to send you a message. Key point: a simple and well designed Web form is easier and quicker to use than an email program.

Don't ask for too much information though: visitors may feel this is too intrusive. Striving to find the right balance is always a worthwhile effort. The ultimate level of your Web success is more often than not determined in the details.

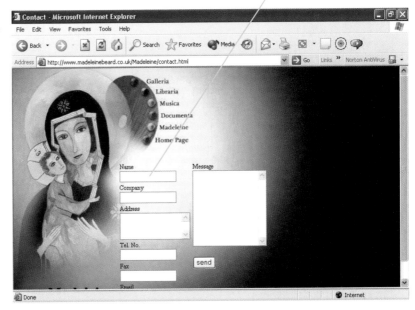

Web forms: top design hints and tips

1 Test a newly designed form using several different Web browsers to ensure maximum compatibility.

2 You can easily set up a form to handle simple enquiries, sign up for an ezine, or to gain feedback information. Your ISP or Web host may provide a form script that exactly meets your needs! However, you'll probably need to enter the email address to which you want the form information sent.

3 You can include a separate form "inside" another so each form collects and sends distinct information to the server. Although a powerful technique, nesting forms in this way can sometimes confuse visitors and is therefore probably best avoided, unless you have a strong reason to include multiple forms.

Adding pizazz to your Web form buttons

If you want to add a little uniqueness to your form design, instead of using the usual boring gray-colored Submit buttons, consider using an image button instead. Here's the code you need to use:

When you establish a website, always keep in mind that you are essentially serving a global group of visitors, and yet this "group" is made up of individuals. Therefore, you're really seeking to capture the hearts and minds of each individual visitor, one at a time. Individuals matter, they are the "details" that collectively can help make your site a roaring success.

1 Create your button images in a program like Paint Shop Pro, NetStudio, Photoshop or Fireworks.

2 Then, instead of using the usual HTML code:

<INPUT type="submit" value="Subscribe">

enter the following:

<INPUT TYPE="image" value="Subscribe" SRC="images/subscribe.gif">

Remember: substitute the example SRC path above with yours, so that it points to where your new Subscribe button (or other button) image is located. In our example, we have put "subscribe.gif" in a folder called "images".

Designing your Web pages

Just adding some text and one or two ill-considered pictures doesn't create an effective Web page. In this chapter, we cover the essentials that you need to know and how to create some special types of Web pages.

Covers

Chapter Thirteen

Creating effective Web page titles

The title of a Web page is what appears in the Browser window Title bar when you access a Web page. The Web page title is nowadays *absolutely essential* to the ranking of a website in search engines and directories. Consider yours carefully.

To help get best results in the search engines listings, keep your title between 50–70 characters in length and place it immediately after the opening <HEAD> tag and before any META descriptions, keywords, and especially before any JavaScript code.

The power words: "You", "New" and "Free" almost always get our attention. Use them often in your Web pages for best results.

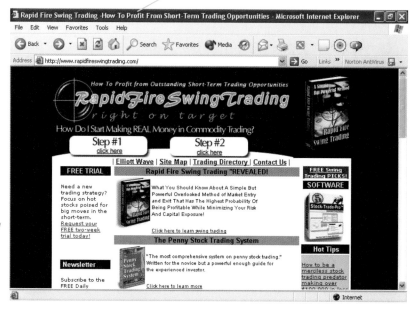

Key point: try to make your first word low in the Alphabet or as close to "A" as possible. Some search engines may use alphabetical listing systems, so "A"s get listed first etc. Unfair, I know...

<u>MOST IMPORTANT</u>: Make sure your title fulfils the following conditions: (1) it's meaningful, (2) it contains your Number 1 search keyword for that page (see the facing page) but *not* the first word in your title and (3) it describes your Unique Selling Proposition (USP) – i.e. it clearly and quickly demonstrates why someone should choose or buy from you above anyone else.

Creating your Web page titles

Consider the following page title: "Welcome to gardening.com". This contains 24 characters including spaces (excluding quotes included here for clarity); it's short, snappy but doesn't include a key benefit.

Perhaps a better title could be: "Access free gardening tips and great value gardening supplies". Although longer with 61 characters including spaces, this title is arguably more meaningful and includes TWO key BENEFITS (visitors buy into benefits).

Search engines: top keyword tips

Basic keyword information provided in these few pages is regularly repackaged with a suit and tie by Internet consultants for hundreds of times the cost of this book, and most websites still don't apply such simple and careful techniques! Your astute book choice now puts you as a Web designer in an incredibly unique and powerful position, but ONLY if you apply these techniques. Congratulations!

Here's why you should usually use phrases instead of single words. Current search engines can pick out single words but can't intelligently put together phrases made up of your single words. However, watch this space: while one expert states something as impossible, another stubborn person is busy trying to work out how to do the impossible.

1 Arrange keywords/phrases in order of importance, the most important first, separated by commas, *no spaces between keywords*; shortened example: <META name="keywords" content="free help,online marketing,internet marketing">.

2 Make sure the first 200 words of text on your page contain the keywords you use in: (1) your Web page title, (2) description and (3) keywords as described in this section.

3 Choose keywords carefully! Make a "rough" list of the kinds of words and phrases you think people might enter in a search engine to find your website. Include some common misspellings (many people have problems with spelling); also consider international spelling differences.

4 Make a "fine" list of about 40–50. Then choose about 10 from that list that you consider are the most important. Keep a copy of both lists in a plain text (.txt) file on your PC's hard drive: then you have easy access for copy/pasting later.

5 When possible, use keyword phrases and plurals instead of single words: "consultants" is better than "consultant". Why? Because "consultants" will catch "consultant", "consult" and "consultants". Get the idea? A little extra forethought is worthwhile here.

6 Appreciate that you can dilute your keyword mix simply by having too many! Have as few keywords as you can. Why? The more keywords you have, the higher the relevance each remaining keyword may be given in a search engine.

7 ESSENTIAL: Don't repeat a keyword more than once. Search engines may consider this action to be keyword spamming and automatically heavily reduce your ranking.

8 Avoid putting banners, tables, graphics or any other "obstacles" at the top of a page: put keyword-rich text there instead.

Creating compelling content

Essentially a website is a just another type of publication: an electronic brochure. So what you put in makes a difference. Consider thinking of your website not as a website, but as a stimulating visitor experience! This might seem like an unlikely proposition, but there are websites out there doing just that!

Generally, people don't like to read text on a screen – if given the choice. Therefore, simply work with this trait and aim to keep text paragraphs brief, clear and to the point.

Key point: if your *target* visitors find your Web pages interesting, attractive and compelling, they're more likely to revisit and recommend your site to others. If they revisit, you have further chances to state your case, start a dialog, make a friend, or close a sale. And personal recommendations are always the best way to build trust.

Deciding what to include in your pages

Once you've clearly established your marketing goals and developed a plan, consider the following ideas:

1 Visitors read only what interests them or is relevant to them. Design your pages to match. Headlines are very important.

2 Try to provide some free content: the word FREE is magnetic, has a lot of power and people just love it! Free causes traffic.

Include a brief description for each image used: search engines can "see" the contents of the ALT tags in images (Chapter 7).

3 Create attractive content that is appropriate for your target visitors.

4 Experiment with ideas to describe your products and services in a compelling and eye-catching way.

5 Empty space on a Web page can work for you – the "considered" choice of empty space is not empty but "active".

6 Although lots of attention-seeking components are available, sometimes a clean, uncluttered Web page can carry its own message.

7 Avoid overloading a page with too much information. If necessary, spread the information across several pages.

Using humor

Jokes and cartoons can add final touches to a Web page – or form the central theme of a website if you're in the laughter business. However, humor needs careful handling. Consider the following:

The Home/Index page represents an ideal starting point at which to fire peoples' imaginations, engage their brains, provide drama or make an impact!

1 To encourage feedback, you could try monthly joke contests with prizes – ideally products from the website – for the winners.

2 Or perhaps a competition to find the funniest, most unusual, or striking email address.

3 Here's another successful idea: invite visitors to email, in 50 words or less, why they deserve a free [product]. Then publish the results. Some hilarious offerings could be forwarded in these situations offering high entertainment value to all concerned.

4 Treat humor-based content with special respect: your brand of humor may not be shared by others. What you consider funny, some might see as offensive. Consider feelings. If you're unsure, get second opinions, or simply choose another approach.

A generic Home/Index page

A Home page is a little like the front door of your house: one of the first things your visitor sees when they log on to your website. Your Home/Index page should clearly state within the first paragraph what your website is about. For businesses, a Home page can also be likened to the front cover of a brochure.

The Home/Index page is the best place to remind visitors to bookmark your site. In fact, why not remind them in several additional places as well?

Deciding what to include in a Home page is crucial. We may be tempted to include far more than perhaps we should. In fact, often we can create a better Home page by establishing what to leave out *after* deciding what we think we need to include.

To avoid overloading visitors with too much clutter at "your front door", limit the number of distinct information chunks to no more than 10 – fewer if possible. This helps create a feeling of space and puts over a sense of planned expectation. Consider also:

Ideally, create a browser-independent website. But if specific types of browser are essential to view your website, tell your visitors which browser(s) work best when viewing your Web pages.

Remember, your Home/Index page is a kind of filter to the other pages that make up your website. Clear the pathways.

2 If possible, include an ezine sign-up box, a guestbook link or a feedback link box. Or consider other ways in which you can capture a visitor's email address.

A personal Home page

A "personal" Web page performs a different purpose to that of club or business-related websites, and should therefore include only relevant components appropriate to their design.

Some of the best Web pages have been developed by individuals who want to promote their hobby or interest and connect with other like-minded individuals. In this way, the Web can produce and stimulate the development of many smaller "communities".

Your Web space may not cost anything if you already have an email account!
Many Internet Service Providers make some free Web space available for you to use should you choose to. Speak to your ISP for details. This kind of Web space may be all you need, and might be ideal for personal or club sites.

This deceptively simple yet cleverly designed fast-loading Home page provides three important key components: an attractive text title, a humanizing component and a tempting invitation to connect

Creating a twenty-four hour online CV/Résumé

In a personal website, you can let your creative flair blossom. In fact, some individuals use a personal website as a kind of curriculum vitae. Many others at least include their CV/Résumé as one of their Web pages. An online CV/Résumé can provide a powerful demonstration of your abilities and imagination. If you include a photo, capture the real you: consider using a photo that puts over warmth. A passport-type photo may not achieve this goal!

1 A simple design succeeds in putting over validity for a Résumé/CV page.

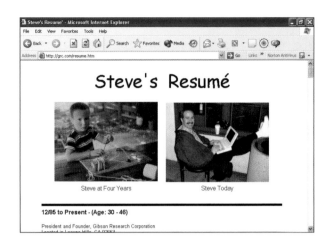

2 The author prefers a more artistic, creative approach than this.

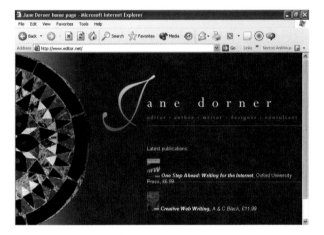

Borrow from business: adopt a theme

When designing a personal website, remember that, although visitors will probably expect you to talk about yourself often, the last thing they want to read is lots of *"I's"*. One way to avoid this situation is to design your Web pages around a theme.

For example, this could be the place where you live or a keen hobby or interest. In this way, you can captivate visitors by introducing the things that interest you before mentioning something about yourself. The more attractive or unusual your theme, the more compelling it can be.

Deciding what to include

For a personal website, you can establish what to put in your Web pages by answering two key questions: why are you providing a personal Web presence and who is the website designed to serve?

Consider the following general guidelines on what to include:

- Your name plus address and qualifications if relevant.

- A good quality photograph of yourself, one that is special and not a passport-type photo. If the emphasis is on your career, consider discussing this with a professional photographer.

- First paragraph: state the purpose of your Web page. Visitors who mistakenly navigate to your site won't waste time (and clog up your site) by having to read further.

- If you want others to contact you, display essential contact information clearly. Include this information on each page.

- Make sure visitors can navigate easily through your website.

- Make your site interesting, engaging and above all individual. On the Internet, it's essential to differentiate yourself from everyone else. Build in lots of variety.

Change your content regularly and let people know that you update regularly. Ideally, include a "What's New" type page. A site that becomes known for regularly providing fresh content helps keep your website in your visitors' "top of mind awareness" zone. Powerful and effective! Yet simple.

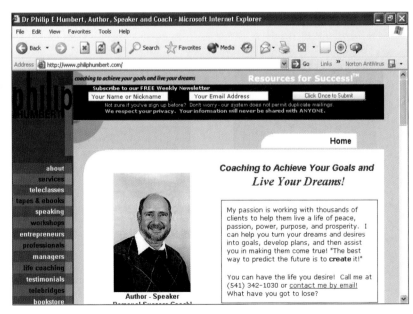

Creating supplementary pages

When considering the design aspects of supplementary pages (that is, those which link back to the Home page) try to create a consistent design style throughout all your pages. Here's why:

When naming your pages, make sure all your page names are in lowercase: some Web host servers are case-sensitive. INDEX.HTML may not be considered the same as index.html or Index.html.

- Consistency provides an increased awareness that your visitors are still on the same website.

- Familiar signposts help visitors know where their location is.

The power of colors, text styles and orientation

Why not consider a specific color for page titles, another for subheadings, another for style of body text and so on, across all of your pages? Visitors then know what to expect. Here's another design orientation tip: place common design elements like logos, buttons or other icons in the same place from page to page.

Saying goodbye to "Under Construction" signs

Avoid using "Under Construction" signs. An unfinished page demonstrates little credibility. If a page is not ready, wait until it's complete before uploading to your website. As a last resort, if you absolutely have to publish an unfinished page, sometimes the best approach is to simply don't advertise the fact that it is unfinished.

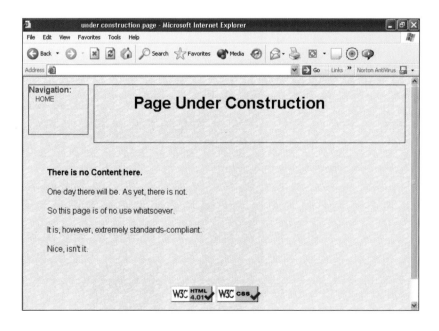

Providing a FAQ page

People buying products and services may have many questions to ask before deciding to buy. If you're designing a website that includes some level of customer support, sometimes a single Web page dedicated to answering Frequently Asked Questions (FAQs) can be a valuable aid for your visitors whilst saving you a lot of extra work. Some of the benefits of providing FAQ files include:

Microsoft FrontPage and NetObjects Fusion both include a template or Wizard that makes creating a FAQ page easy.

- They can overcome possible objections to a sale without requiring direct contact (instant cost saving).

- They demonstrate that detailed consideration has been given to customers' needs right from the outset.

- They can provide a greater range of information enabling customers to make better buying decisions.

- They can reduce the need for after-sales problem-solving support as basic questions can be answered in advance.

Creating a FAQ list

If you can provide FAQ lists, it's usually a good idea to do so. The cost of Web space, compared with more traditional advertising media, is low and so this method offers real value for money in addition to providing quick help for visitors.

1. Think of common questions visitors might ask and then clearly document both the questions with the answers. If, during this exercise, other possible questions emerge, don't worry: by providing the answers, you're actually making the buying decision easier for your customers.

2. If necessary, interview sales and support staff who regularly deal with these kinds of problems to learn about the kind of questions visitors might ask.

3. Save, edit, check and convert the FAQ file to HTML format and include it within your website.

4. Provide a link to the FAQ file, possibly on the Home page and maybe other appropriate pages too. Make sure visitors know about your FAQ pages.

Using Web page templates

For larger websites containing many pages, the easiest way to be consistent in design across all the pages is to use templates which include all the repeated elements you want to include on every page. Here's how to work with Web page templates:

Some of the best Web design software (like Microsoft FrontPage, Macromedia Dreamweaver, NetObjects Fusion and HotMetal Pro) provide many different Web page and website templates that can save you hours of additional work.

1 First, identify all the Web page components you want to include in a template.

2 Next, create a Web page that contains all these components and save it as a template. Or simply store the page in a location that you reserve for your Web templates.

3 When you're ready to create a page based on the template, open the template and immediately save it to another name (so you don't delete your original template with the changes you're about to make).

4 You can then modify the page to include all the essential details for the current page, then re-save.

5 Repeat Steps 3 and 4 for all the other pages you want created.

Some of the more powerful Web design software packages (like Macromedia Dreamweaver) can seem intimidating to new users, while other types (like NetObjects Fusion) may seem simpler. Try out various packages, then choose one. Give yourself the time you need to become familiar with it. Don't rush and don't expect to know it all at once. Have fun but don't be afraid to make mistakes and you'll almost certainly learn more quickly.

Routing to browser-specific pages

Some sophisticated Web pages may not display properly even on the most common Web browsers. However, by applying some simple techniques you can perform a check on a browser when it tries to access your Web page/site; then, if the browser is not compatible with that page, you can reroute the visitor to a page that is compatible with their browser. This way, most visitors see your pages as you intended them to be seen. The drawback is of course more work for you and possibly the need to create another set of Web pages.

The free "Browser-Matcher" script checks which browser a visitor is using and then redirects the visitor to the browser-compatible page you create. Check it out at: www.citro.net/scripts/more.shtml#browse.

Using JavaScript to detect JavaScript-compatible browsers

Early browsers did not support JavaScript. If your default pages contain JavaScript and these older browsers were to try and view them, an error message would almost certainly be displayed – not a good start for a new visitor.

Adapt the code below to detect the version of JavaScript you want to optionally reroute a visitor to another page. Set the minimum version of JavaScript you want to check for in "LANGUAGE=". If that condition is met, the visitor is rerouted to the "welcome2.html" page, otherwise, the message between <H3> and </H3> is shown below:

To edit your HTML pages and include JavaScript, I recommend you don't use word processor software. Why? To avoid the risk of saving the file in the software's native format, rather than .htm or .html. Use a pure text editor like TextPad (Helios Software Solutions: www.textpad.com).

```
<HTML>
<HEAD>
<TITLE>For JavaScript-compatible browsers</TITLE>
<SCRIPT LANGUAGE="JAVASCRIPT1.2"
TYPE="TEXT/JAVASCRIPT">
<!--Hides this script from older browsers
window.location="welcome2.html"
// End of hiding script from older browsers -->
</SCRIPT>
</HEAD>
<BODY BGCOLOR="BLUE">
<H3>Your Web browser is not compatible with the latest version of JavaScript. You can upgrade using this link...</H3>
</BODY>
</HTML>
```

Creating 3D Web pages

Most websites currently display in two dimensions, often using a newsletter-type delivery approach. However, we see, touch and think in 3D, so it's natural to extend this to a Web page.

Arranging to view in 3D reintroduces depth and brings us back to what are arguably more natural surroundings.

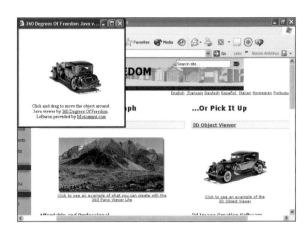

For visitors to benefit fully from 3D, a relatively fast PC is usually desirable. I suggest (as a minimum) a 133 MHz Pentium-type PC with at least 32 Mb of RAM. Fortunately, most PCs and Apple Macs now come with at least 64Mb of RAM.

This has benefits for Web page designers: having the capability to view an object (and then turn it around to examine what it looks like from all angles) provides a much better picture of that object.

For some complex objects, the ability to move in 3D could be considered essential – medical uses, for example. The all-encompassing term "object", used above, could of course be modified in other ways for use on a Web page. Consider:

3D, simulated 3D and animated and interactive slide shows can also be created using Flash and AVI technology. For example, StillMotion Creator is one such application. For more information, visit: www. imagematics.com/.

- Taking an imaginary tour around a new type of car engine in a motor company website.

- Examining skeletal structures from all angles in a medical-oriented website.

- Browsing through the aisles of a virtual store, picking up goods and examining them before purchasing.

- Watching a living entity grow and mutate in a Natural History-oriented website.

- Navigating around a large university using a 3D map.

- Moving through the fascinating corridors of a top museum or picture gallery. And so on.

Devising website virtual tours

Flash and 3D perspective animation technology have also created many amazing new possibilities. A popular new trend is to provide interactive virtual tours of buildings, exhibitions, showcase tours around commercial and domestic properties. Using this detailed imagery and high quality technology, vibrant and engaging Web experiences can be created. Typical features include:

- Pan, zoom and rotation of 3D objects.

- Changing direction, changing rooms and viewpoints combining wide angle digital photography techniques, transition effects and animated galleries.

- Design and creation of floor animation plans.

- Creation of AVI videos from a series of still images. Photos can be "stitched" together seamlessly to create panoramas and slide shows.

- With the correct production software, visitors won't even need to install any special plug-ins.

- Even hotspots, which can be clicked to move the focal point elsewhere within a virtual image tour, can be created.

To view a superb example of high-quality, engaging design combined with Flash and virtual tour technology, the author recommends you visit www.tyburnconvent.org.uk as shown here.

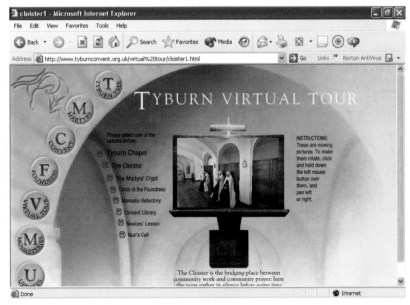

An example: Three Sixty Degrees of Freedom

At: http://www.360dof.com, you can see an ideal example of what is possible when using cost-effective powerful tools to create 3D and panoramic virtual tours. Features include:

- Combines scalable 3D objects and rotate in a virtual tour.

- Cross-browser and cross-platform support. Plug-ins not required.

- A range of plain English tutorials, hints, tips and tricks.

- Uses Apple QuickTime VR format.

- No special Web design skills necessary to install the items.

- Works on Windows and Macintosh Internet Explorer and Netscape browsers from version 3 and later.

- Developer Suite contains all that you need to create 3D and virtual tours from your own source material.

- A range of 15 Panorama template websites that also use JavaScript techniques, buttons, lists and forms.

An excellent example of virtual tour technology can be seen at: www.english-country-cottages.co.uk, from which visitors can actually look around a holiday home before deciding to book their holiday.

The Developer Suite uses either Java or Flash technology and, when combined with JavaScript techniques, additional innovative special effects can be created.

Creating a superb business website

As businesses have perhaps the most to lose or gain from a website, it's essential to start off properly. In this chapter, we tackle the essential issues head on.

Covers

Chapter Fourteen

The Internet baby has grown up

Almost unknown to the general public, a quiet revolution is happening. The following trends demonstrate huge potential:

- Broadband households worldwide. In 2001 the figure was 12 million; early in 2003, it was 43 million!

- Wireless Internet subscribers. In 2001 there were 40 million; in 2003, there are 350 million!

- Total number of Web pages. In 2001 there were 6 billion; in 2003, there are 16 billion!

Why establish a business website?

Web businesses have reasons to be cheerful. These include:

- There's a global reach; no national boundaries apply.

- No premises or similar rental costs are required.

- Low overheads: Web space is cheap! Use of Content Management Systems can dramatically reduce update costs.

- A business can be open 24 hours a day, every day.

- *Total* visitor attention (unlike standard sales environments).

- Sales can be increased cost-effectively.

- Gain a competitive edge: set up an *effective* website before your competitors!

- The Web and email definitely cut marketing costs.

- Creating Web-based corporate catalogues means fewer conventional printed versions may be needed.

- Many Internet users are affluent: a website provides a direct link to these potentially lucrative customer profiles.

- Incentives/promotions can be tested quickly and cheaply.

- Certain niche products which can't be sold cost-effectively by traditional methods may be viable on the Internet because of the low setup costs combined with low day-to-day running costs and the powerful global reach of the Internet.

If you provide professional advice, seriously consider getting Professional Indemnity insurance to protect yourself from possible lawsuits. The global nature of the Web means legal repercussions of any dispute may not be clear-cut.

If possible, try to register several variations of your domain name, especially common misspellings. The small cost outlay for getting a domain name will almost certainly pay for itself, when you consider the possible loss of business that might result otherwise.

Establishing your domain name

What is a domain name?

A domain name is the online equivalent of a postal/mail address. Web businesses need a businesslike identity. This starts with getting a "true" domain name. Examples of "true" domain names include: ineasysteps.com, caade.net and AustinHall.co.uk. When you add "http://www." to the front of a domain name, you have a full Web address (also referred to as a URL).

Get a true domain name

Maybe not all the best domain names are taken! Network Solutions (USA) repossess thousands due to nonpayment. For a tiny fee you can have a list of these names emailed to you. Check out: www. unclaimeddomains.com/.

A "true" domain name is much better than one derived from an Internet Service Provider's address. Consider the following two examples; one is easier to remember: www.InternetTIPS.com or, http://ourworld.compuserve.com/homepages/internettips/.

Key point: Usually, the shorter your domain name, the better. Include your domain name on all business stationery. When ready, tell as many people as possible about your Web address. For international organizations, ".com" (company/organization) is the best choice. However, you could also register ".net" and ".co.uk" or other country variations if they're still available.

How to reserve a domain name

If possible, consider registering names which sound similar to your "main" domain (to prevent organizations that you may not want to be associated with using them). Your potential clients may enter similar-sounding names to find you as a first measure, rather than using a search engine, simply because this approach is easier.

1 Check if the domain name you want is available (no one else has already claimed it). Visit your favorite domain name provider or Internet Service Provider. For example: http://www.register.com/ You may be able to save money by shopping around.

2 If the domain name you want is still available, register it quickly! Usually, you'll need to register your new domain name for at least the first 2 years.

3 For .co.uk domains, if you're based in the UK, you could see what your Internet Service Provider can offer, or perhaps use Nominet in the UK at www.nic.uk/.

4 Keep the confirmation emails you receive after registration in a safe place for your business records and proof of ownership.

Web business guidelines

In business, small businesses have most to gain from creating an effective website. Even a tiny business can project a Web image as well as, or better than, a huge international company.

For businesses, the Web Search engines and Directories can provide access to a vast range of business information; enable users to research existing and new markets; and even provide information about competitors.

Setting up a corporate website however, is much more complex. For example, many companies have a clearly defined policy regarding the use of logos and other corporate graphic styles. Therefore, this and other such aspects should be considered early in your website design as part of an overall design plan.

Also, corporate sites need to be sure that access to the website doesn't provide a weak link to often priceless information. An effective firewall can protect a network from unauthorized access. Set up and maintenance costs can also be high. See www.grc.com.

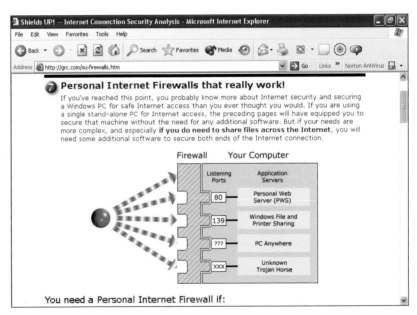

Established businesses setting up a Web presence should consider employing experts to create a new Web brand image. Branding is often considered to be an essential component of any successful Internet business – even tiny Web ventures need a unique identity, a brand.

Most importantly, "Make a plan, or plan to fail" so the saying goes. For a website, it's even more true! Make a Web business plan (initial setup) and a Web marketing plan (day-to-day planning). Here's the most important requirement for any Web business: make your site look AND perform in an absolutely professional manner. Over-deliver on expectations and you'll stand out!

A smart business start-up plan?

Included here for entertainment purposes only, the following viewpoint shows how one entrepreneur approaches the basics:

"Don't do anything you don't have to do until you have made the first sale. Setting up a corporation, buying insurance, and getting your local status secured is a crazy waste of time for a start-up operator. Prove to yourself and anyone who might want to invest in you that your brilliant idea works. Do that by making a sale!

After you have made the first sale, make another one. And then another. Don't print business cards. Don't worry about stationery. Just keep making sales. You need the cash for the next step.

Once you are confident you can make a sale and have proven that your idea is profitable (i.e. you get paid more than you spend), you have to design a marketing program so you can roll out the selling process indefinitely. This involves advertising. Direct-response advertising is best. Base your plan on someone else's success. Don't reinvent the wheel.

Don't worry about notifying regulators and government agencies that you are going to start a business. All they want to do is control and monitor you. Since your business isn't going yet … since it has no cash flow … it's not really a business. There will be plenty of time to get yourself hamstrung with regulations later. Follow the law, but don't be foolish.

Buy business cards and/or stationery only if and when you actually need them. This time may never come. I run and/or own at least a half-dozen multimillion-dollar businesses and have neither a card nor stationery for any of them."

© 2003, ETR LLC, Early to Rise, 245 NE 4th Ave., Suite 102 Delray Beach, FL 33483, USA

When thinking about the design of your pages, take a look at what your competitors are doing. This doesn't mean copy their Web content, but it does at least let you know what you've got to beat to "steal their thunder".

Some Web stores may not even need an inventory. When a customer orders, the Web store contacts its supplier who can send the goods direct to the customer.

"Early to Rise" is a free daily e-letter service for those of us who aspire to a better, more enriched life. It's written by a successful multimillionaire entrepreneur who's also an experienced educator and motivator. You can sign-up here: www.EarlyToRise.com/LifeSuccess.htm

The first 60 seconds!

Many people now live a "push-button" way of life. We like instant results and these reactions are transferred to the Web. We simply don't like waiting; we want it and we want it now! Whether this trait is good or bad is beside the point: certainly, the first 60 seconds after a visitor enters your website address can make or break its success. Aim to surprise and delight new visitors.

Keep the Home/Index page download time to a minimum. If you can do this so that a site loads in under 10 seconds using a 28.8 modem, wonderful! However, under 25 or 30 seconds – or even more – may be tolerated if perceived expectations are high. Deliver on those expectations to win the Web business game.

For left-to-right readers, the higher up the page you place your ezine (email newsletter) subscription box, the more likely subscribers are to see it, possibly leading to more sign-ups.

Key point: the left uppermost area of your Web page naturally draws the eye, so has special influence for left-to-right readers.

Installing an ezine subscription box

The most important purpose a business website can fulfil is to first capture targeted email addresses. With an email address AND permission to contact, you always have a second chance to sell a product or service. If he or she signs up to receive an email newsletter, or regular updates, special offers, or whatever, you have repeated chances to sell. When someone who knows the product or service you're providing leaves an email address, there's a good chance that this person is a hot prospect for what you're offering.

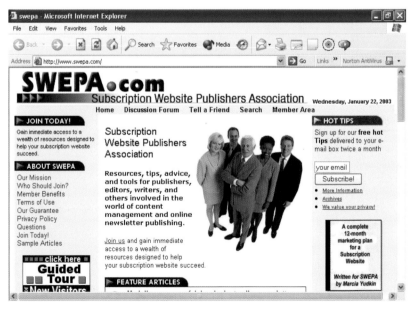

Building credibility and trust

"Only scam and con artists sell on the Web" – an untrue phrase but one that with over-hyped media exposure creates great Sunday reading! Web shoppers are the most cautious buyers. To succeed as a respectable website owner, you have to fight the false but common misperceptions among the global general public and prove yourself. After all, why should they trust you *before* they get to know you? Actively and regularly show honesty and integrity to gain the trust of visitors. To help think up ideas, let's take a brief look at some positive reasons why people do buy on the Web.

Recent statistics from www.clickz. com/ suggest that 64% of current online sales are abandoned before being completed. Don't be amongst these: make your order process simple, reliable and trustworthy.

Evaluating why people buy over the Web

People buy from a Web store for many reasons. However, often there's *one important reason above all others* which affects their buying decision. From a Web page design standpoint, we could benefit by identifying some of the more important reasons why people are motivated enough to complete the buying process from a Web store. Consider:

- Price, quality, branding, and usefulness.

- Perceived value.

- Some folks can simply be so entranced by a Web presentation they buy through the impulse mood that buying creates.

If you can meet that last condition above, you'll be envied by peers and competitors alike – it's the hardest one to achieve.

Guidelines that can help build a great reputation

Although businesses can address the "open 24 hours" issue using answering machines and automated voice systems, it's well known that customers can become irritated with automated replies, possibly leading to lost sales.

1 Create a Web Privacy policy and Terms of Business page. Make sure visitors know about it and have easy access to it.

2 Protect your visitors' email addresses and other personal details and make it known in several places that you do this. If you say you don't share this information with other parties, stick to your claims: demonstrate integrity.

3 Use a secure server to handle Web credit card transactions. More about this important topic later in this chapter.

Developing a theme-based approach

A website designed around a theme tends to draw more targeted, "pre-qualified" visitors, while matching preferred search engine requirements for better ranking. This approach also aims to filter out visitors who may be just browsing or curious or just looking for something for free (none of which contribute to sales).

Visitor numbers may be fewer, but a higher percentage stand to buy something at some stage. With highly relevant content, great offers and a compelling call to action, you can get more sales!

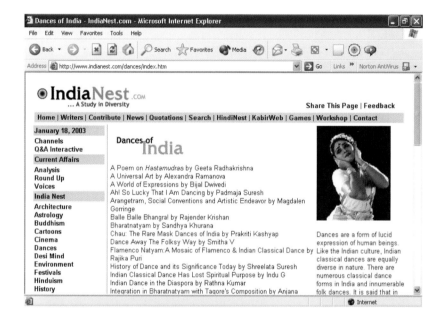

A website reflects the company as a whole. A "bad" website can thus undo years of previous successes – or worse!

Assessing the competition

To stand out from the crowd, you need to know just what the "crowd" is doing on their websites. Therefore, with a list of competitors' websites prepared, use your Web browser and see how the competition performs:

*   Note which Web components gain your attention and why.

*   Also, note down those components and elements that irritate you or cause problems for your browser. This kind of information could be useful in establishing what not to include in your own Web pages.

Using doorway pages

A doorway or hook is a Web page you create (containing a carefully crafted individual title, META description and META keywords – Chapter 13) that only links to the "main" website Home/Index page. The "main" Home/Index pages should not contain any links that point back to any doorway pages. You submit doorway pages to the search engines in the normal way. Doorway pages can only be "seen" by the search engines, not by visitors, and that's the point: they're designed to increase your exposure to the search engines.

If you decide to use doorway pages, use them with care and consideration. Why? Some search engines may consider doorway pages as spamming, so always check the details to ensure you abide by search engine rules and regulations.

However, do make sure that doorway pages are acceptable to a search engine. Make sure you don't break any engine usage rules.

A power strategy

Here's a potentially highly profitable, perfectly reasonable, ethical strategy that could provide maximum value from the search engines if you have some spare funds available.

Instead of having just a single domain name, get several (all similar, if possible). Install your website on each and set up links between them all, so that each domain "points" to each of the others. Modify the content of each site if you have a range of product/service lines and, if possible, group each single product or service into a single domain. Ensure your content concentrates on that product or service only.

Doorway pages can work best when they point to different products or services on multiple websites or domains in which each website concentrates on a single product or service. Such doorway pages can almost act like a mini site – and therefore are more likely to be "accepted" by search engines.

Let's see how this could work. Imagine you have 8 domain names/ websites with about 10 pages in each site. Now add about 30 doorway pages as described above to each site. So each site now has about 40 pages over 8 domains giving you 320 pages working for you in the search engines/directories. Compare that to your original 10 pages with a single website!

Why is the number of pages so important? Part of the ranking mechanism in many search engines is how many other pages link to a website: 320 pages linked together probably rank better than 10 pages. It's that simple!

Creating doorway pages

You can create doorway pages manually, or via your Web submission/design software. NetObjects Fusion users can purchase the MultiDoor Component from http://club.coolmaps.com to automate the task, saving many hours.

Implementing the 2-Step plan

Effective Web pages can be created more easily by creating and following a basic plan. For example, why not:

Setting up an effective website has got to be good for business. However, a poorly maintained site can pull the stature of an existing business down surprisingly quickly.

1 Get into the "high-quality" mindset. Like a master carpenter, pay attention to the details. Don't compromise. Test continually.

2 Then, look for ways in which you can *add extra tangible value*; something that really matters to your potential customers.

Step 1 above is self-evident and is achieved through care, consideration and lots of testing. Real world examples for meeting the Step 2 condition are covered in various sections in this book. Other ideas for Step 2 could include:

- Create a virtual hook by providing genuinely valuable free information or key advice.

- Include plenty of options for customer feedback.

- Create a "What's New" or "Latest Freebies" page.

- Provide a link to your company newsletter (printable).

Selling a product or service? Why not present brief details of the core subject (don't overload visitors) with "click" access to lots of backup information using links. Provide this information in a clear, unbiased, sober and factual way using familiar examples where possible.

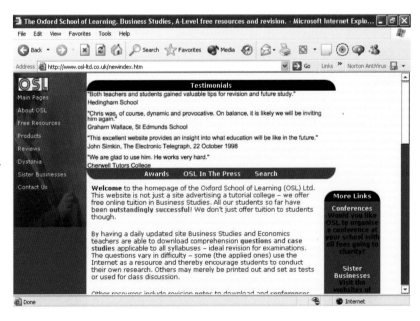

Using profit-creating "magic" words

Words can sell your product or compel a visitor to contact you by phone, fax or person-to-person. Words are powerful, but recent statistics indicate that five times as many people read headlines as body copy!

Carefully combining headlines with associated graphics and layout can essentially sell your product. The rest is support or detail material only. So what do we want from headlines and body copy? Answer: to grab their attention! You can do this using strong, powerful action-motivated words and phrases. Consider the following guidelines:

"Show, don't tell." Sound advice. Why? Showing how or why something is the way it is, is more credible than simply telling someone it's better because you say it is! In this way, you're stating your case with evidence instead of simply delivering an online speech.

1 Your headlines are crucial to your success. Include *a strong benefit that is relevant to your visitors* and which makes them stop whatever they're doing and compels them to want to discover more now!

2 Consider using the three top power words: YOU, NEW and FREE – the most powerful attention "getters".

3 Consider including other emotive action words and phrases like: Absorbing, Absolutely, Advice, Amazing, Announcing..., At Last..., Bargains, Boom..., Breakthrough, Compelling, Convincing, Discover, Do You..., Easy, Energizing, Fascinating, Finally, Growth, Guarantee, Hate, Health, Here, How much..., How to..., How would..., Interesting, Last Minute..., Love, Luxury, Money, Obsession, Only, Protect, Proven, Results, Rewards, Safety, Sale..., Save, Secrets of..., Security, Share, Show me..., Starter Kit..., The Truth Of... Unique, Useful, Valuable, Yes....

4 Experiment. Keep records of the results you get. Think very carefully before changing a successful headline just because you think it's time for a change.

5 Create compelling reasons why visitors should buy *now*, not later. Make time-dependent offers; be seen to stick to them.

Providing incredible value

To entice visitors to go to a Web page *and* to keep them coming back repeatedly requires a special kind of thinking. Firstly, when visitors log on to a website, remember they're spending in at least three ways:

- The time needed to visit your website.

- The time lost through not performing another activity whilst they're online.

- The cost involved in setting up a Web browser and in maintaining an Internet link (online costs).

Whenever possible, liberally display verifiable testimonials from previously satisfied customers (but get permission first).

Visitors therefore must feel they're getting value from their Web surfing investment. One way to meet this need is to be seen to be providing extra value; be different. **Key hint:** find the one thing that makes your organization absolutely unique and build on it like crazy in your website!

Experiment with ideas: test, measure and modify

Here are some real-world examples. Consider:

- An online music store could provide some free downloads (resolve copyright issues first though).

- A bookstore could give away a free choice of book up to a certain value when a customer places an order above a specific quantity or order value.

- A consultant or market research organization could provide free information sheets covering key advice on specific topics. This is probably better done using an autoresponder rather than a Web page, so you can capture valuable targeted email addresses.

- An accountancy website could provide some free information on a range of topics. Perhaps change the topic once weekly/monthly to heighten interest.

- Press releases could be provided at strategic times giving up-to-the minute information on new products, services or developments which might be of interest to customers.

Effective advertising on the Web

Web advertising costs can be much lower compared to traditional media, and advertising space on the Web is not in short supply (yet). To be effective, Web adverts need to be attractive, relevant, compelling, clear and quick to load for the following groups:

One of the most influential positions on a Web page is the upper left corner, as our eyes are naturally drawn to this location at first glance.

- Information seekers.

- Individuals who are cost-conscious.

- Number seekers: those who benefit from viewing statistics, graphs and charts.

- People who are more likely to be motivated to action through a graphically-rich Web design environment.

- Those who are first and foremost quality-conscious and value-oriented.

- People who particularly enjoy audiovisual content.

One of the most powerful advertising techniques is to use movement and an eye-catching color scheme. Web multimedia (the combination of text, graphics, animation, video and sound) makes maximum use of this approach in progressive advertising.

If your organization has received positive press coverage, why not refer to this information in a website (see the Press Releases tab on the right)? In business, you need all the PR you can get; don't hide your gems away. Furthermore, respected independent praise or implied endorsement can be a powerful sales aid.

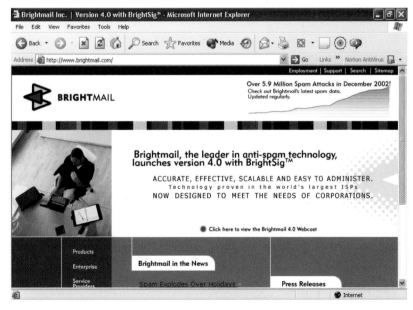

Guiding visitors with a website tour

If you're providing a website tour, create drama; make an impact; stimulate your visitors' imaginations with pleasing sights and sounds. Evoke the sensations of touch and smell by drawing on memorable experiences. Use carefully crafted words as discussed.

For any website to be a success, it needs to be actively AND consistently promoted at every opportunity using conventional AND unconventional channels.

Get creative; try to think of a new "angle" on which to promote your site. The media is crying out for stories that are interesting to their readers, so provide a "story" they want (not one that uses blatant self-promotion) and you'll probably get all the free PR you can handle.

Spend the time you need to leave a lasting favorable impression. Clearly put over the benefits you're providing. In your closing sequence, prompt your visitors to action: to order a product, leave an email address, fill in a form, or commit to revisiting.

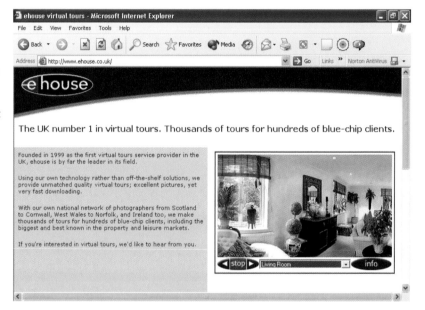

The importance of branding

Many experts agree that a strong brand name, promoted equally strongly on Web pages, provides one of the most essential ingredients for achieving a successful Web trading experience.

For smaller companies or organizations, don't aim to give the impression of being a much larger corporation. Web users can probably see through the fabrication eventually, then trust is lost forever. Instead, why not magnify your impact by using your most powerful asset: your uniqueness and flexibility? Build on them.

Designing your business Index page

A Web business needs to convert a browsing prospect into a paying customer for as long as possible. Keeping a business-oriented website up to date with fresh new content added regularly is *essential* to create an interesting, attractive and dynamic experience for visitors. The Home/Index page is the best place to start.

Avoiding reputation melt down

For businesses and organizations, the Home/Index page is the online equivalent of the front door or corporate reception area. The impression created by an Index page in the mind of a new prospect is crucial to your Web success. A poor or ill-considered corporate Index page can damage an organization's reputation quicker than most other ways. Why? The Web provides almost instant feedback. A great promotional tool, but bad news can travel just as fast.

If you include links to other websites, ideally place these links at a dedicated location (or separate page) to reduce the risk of visitors leaving your website erroneously or before you want them to leave. Then, make sure the links you provide open up a new second window, so the original (your site) is still easily available.

People make judgements about the business from what they see (and possibly hear) on your Web pages, the general impression they get, as well as from what other people may say. It's crucial, therefore, that a business-oriented website should favorably reflect the image of the company or organization and the branding of the products and services it represents.

The power of a commercial Index page

The hyperlinks installed in a commercial Index page can provide the key to fast information access. A well thought out Index page can provide visitors with the means to make product comparisons and evaluations, check prices and place orders in minutes instead of hours or days.

An Index page also acts like a signpost, guiding visitors to the desired part of your website. The pointers, therefore, need to be clear, easy to use and direct.

However, one of the most striking characteristics of an Index page is that your visitors always keep control. In a conventional sales presentation, only after the recipients have listened to the entire presentation can they decide what is especially useful. Using the hyperlinks in an Index page, however, visitors can navigate to the areas that interest them almost immediately. This fact has powerful implications from a Web design standpoint.

Here are some ideas of what to include in your Index page:

- Business title: individual or organization name and logo are essential to build a brand.

- Contact details: postal address, phone and fax numbers; email and Web addresses.

Consider placing a special button or icon (for visitors to click) that allows them to quickly insert the email address of someone they know who would also be interested in your site. In fact, why not maximize this opportunity: consider creating space for, say, up to 5 additional friends or other email sources?

- Copyright statement: essential to protect your work.

- A clear index to your site. Perhaps a graphical toolbar-type design approach, or a "looser" pictorial graphic design, or something entirely different.

- Links to other pages in the website: What's New; Products; Services; About Us; Email contacts; etc.

- Links to relevant and thorough information about what you're offering. Provide plenty of background information to support your case, but do so in such a way that visitors can choose whether to view it.

- If you want to provide a dedicated Web form page, ideally include a link to it here.

- Why not include something particularly relevant, eye-catching or stimulating to your visitors, and which can be changed or updated as desired? Example: an eye-catching "What's New" or "What's Hot" link.

- If relevant, why not include a brief company mission statement or a personalized quote from the managing director, chief executive or other leader?

- Possibly include a link to some genuine and verifiable testimonials from satisfied customers – but get their written permission first. If possible, display a recognized seal of trust icon too.

- A link pointing to job openings within the company.

Competitions, prizes and quizzes

Many of us enjoy competitions. But even if we're not competitive, we might like to have a chance at winning a prize. Competitions, draws, quizzes and so on help add special value to a website.

The value of contests

Web page crosswords or similar puzzles can help keep visitors interacting with your website – and possibly buying an additional product as something particularly relevant "catches" their eye. Just make sure that what you do isn't just for fun, but has some measurable commercial value.

Consider the points below in relation to your Web pages:

- Contests can urge people to want to visit and keep revisiting.

- Idea: aim to integrate your product or service as part of a contest. In the "Who did it" style, you could spread strategic "clues" throughout your website to encourage visitors to almost subconsciously take the "fast track" to learn what's on offer in a fun-packed way.

- Ask contest participants to provide information about themselves. Targeted information is one of the main benefits of hosting a contest. Unless someone shouts their name, you don't know they exist! Anything that encourages visitors to say "Hello, I'm here, this is who I am and what I like" has real, lasting commercial value.

Analyzing why visitors revisit

Anything new on your website, whether it be a contest, new product range or service, should also be promoted further using traditional means like press releases, brochures, trade shows, and so on.

- To gain something for free or to save money.

- The Home page has been bookmarked in the visitor's browser. (Always tell visitors to bookmark your page.)

- There's a compelling interactive component: an online game or perhaps relevant, stimulating puzzles.

- To solve a problem, make their job, task or role easier or improve the quality of their life.

- A belief that they are, in some special way, taking part in something bigger, more important than their normal day-to-day activities. The experience of visiting makes them feel good about themselves, by being invited to perhaps contribute in some way or to simply help others.

- The site/page is considered by peers to be "cool".

Introduction to e-commerce

Profiling Web page visitors for business

For anyone selling goods/services on the Web, it's essential to learn more about Web users. Visitors who buy online prefer to do so for several different reasons. For example:

- They like to keep control of the transaction.

- They don't like the hard-sell approach (beware using ill-considered or "unmanaged" popups).

- They don't appreciate uninvited sales attempts.

- They prefer to buy when they're ready, not before.

- They like the option to change their mind without penalty.

- They usually prefer to have access to plenty of relevant background information.

- They may not appreciate uninvited email (known as spam).

Getting ready for e-commerce on your website

If you want to handle money on your website, for secure transactions your Web host must support Secure Socket Layer (SSL) and handle online forms. Different providers use different scripts to handle this kind of information so discuss these aspects with your ecommerce provider at an early stage.

As transaction-type Web pages involve considerably more technical and design input, they can cost more to develop. However, new easy-to-use software packages or ecommerce "plug-ins" are now available. For example, see: www.paypal.com, www.clickbank.com and www.worldpay.com – all ideal for small- and medium-sized businesses to handle Web transactions easily.

Corporate Web transactions

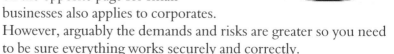

When considering the business of Web transactions, the same advice as provided on the opposite page for small businesses also applies to corporates. However, arguably the demands and risks are greater so you need to be sure everything works securely and correctly.

Setting up a website to accept orders can be both a benefit and a shock, at least initially! Remember, Web businesses are open to a global market 24 hours a day, 7 days a week, all through the year. So you need to be sure that your business can cope with this increased level of exposure.

For large corporate users, considering setting up a website is a particularly important step. If you host the entire operation in-house, costs can be high. Remedy: secure advanced fixed-cost contracts, if possible.

Web credit card transactions

Any business faced with the task of setting up a Web-based display of products with access to a secure ordering facility will normally need to discuss their requirements with people who have skills in database programming, installing a database on a secure server, and ensuring high security applies in the areas of product viewing, ordering and performing transactions.

The Web is part of a fairly new landscape. In this still largely ungoverned "land", the rules are hazy at best. Any business wanting to create a Web presence should make detailed plans and exercise caution when forming new online partnerships or alignments.

Lots of different shopping cart systems are now available for Web businesses. For example, Actinic software (http://www.actinic.com) can help make the job much easier.

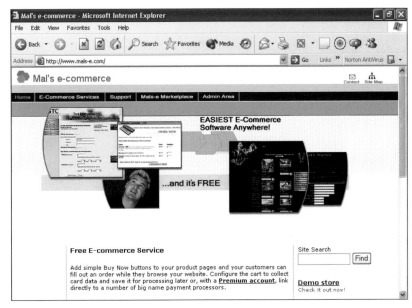

You can design a Web page form to send its information using "standard" email. However, the information is not as secure when compared to using a CGI script. Especially avoid using "standard" email when sending sensitive data. To email more securely, consider checking out services like HushMail at: www.hushmail.com.

Other free, simpler and low-cost shopping cart options are also available through companies like "Mal's e-commerce" at: www.mals-e.com, through which you can set up your online shop to accept secure credit card payments in a range of currencies.

The shopping cart from "Mal's e-commerce" can also "plug in" to a range of popular ecommerce payment gateways – such as those offered by Cybercash, Authorizenet, Internetsecure, Trustcommerce, Verisign, Worldpay, Secpay and others.

Online security: using secure servers

Sending sensitive information like credit card details over the Internet and the Web has been given a massive boost recently by the popular use of secure servers. A secure server is a powerful PC which encrypts sensitive data to keep it private and highly secure.

Here's how to easily identify a secure server: look at the Web address; Look for a "s" after "http", like https://. Ordinary Web addresses start with: http:// whereas secure Web addresses are shown as: https://.

When conventional credit card transactions take place in, for example, a restaurant or retail store, unscrupulous individuals can simply listen carefully and look over a payee's shoulder to gain quite a lot of useful information.

Not so with a secure server! Web transactions carried out through reputable organizations with secure servers are now probably one of the safer ways to pay for goods and services – and the public are coming to realize this as PCs and the Web become tightly integrated into modern living.

What exactly is a secure server?

A server is simply a name given to a powerful PC which serves other PCs in a special way. The "secure" description implies that information moving between the central server and the PCs it serves is protected in some way: usually this is done by encrypting the information to deter unauthorized access. Good idea!

Here's how to identify whether you're connecting through a secure server while using a Netscape Navigator browser: look for either a key or padlock icon situated (usually) at the lower part of the screen. A key appears in unbroken blue for secured connections and broken blue for unsecured links. If a padlock icon is used, when the padlock is closed, the link uses a secure server. When open – like that shown below – the link is insecure:

Why bother providing a secure server?

When sensitive information like credit card details are transferred on the Internet without protection, key information can be used to steal from the credit card holder's account. Although Internet buyers now have better protection from most good credit card companies, a secure server offers better security.

Protecting privacy with encryption technology

The best secure servers use the Secure Sockets Layer (SSL) system. SSL is an encryption technology available on Microsoft Windows and Apple Mac platforms. SSL can use a 128-bit encryption key for international transactions. SSL is really bad news for prospective Internet thieves.

SSL SECURE PAYMENT

Autoresponders: your 24-hour tool

On the Web, people are impatient and first impressions really do count, so it's especially important that you respond quickly and efficiently to enquiries. Autoresponders, one of the most powerful automated Web tools available, can help meet this challenge. Here's how: when someone sends an email to a specific Web address you provide, your autoresponder can reply automatically, usually within seconds or minutes. Smart autoresponders can now also be set to follow up on previous messages several times.

Make email work for you. Failing to reply to an email is like setting up a freephone number and then ignoring the phone when it rings.

Working 24 hours a day even when your PC is switched off, an autoresponder can send your marketing information to potentially tens of thousands of people across the globe. To discover more, type "autoresponder" into your favorite search engine. Consider the following points:

- An autoresponder can save valuable time, especially when designed to answer Frequently Asked Questions.

- You can ensure most questions are answered promptly and properly, or even provide an entire training course.

Email offers superb value for money! If you're in business, why not (after completing a sale and obtaining payment) email a separate "Thank you for your order" message to your customer immediately or definitely within a few days? Or, set up an autoresponder to do it for you.

- With a carefully thought out design, visitors may not even be aware that they are receiving an automated response.

Designing a Web page order form

In some ways, doing business on the Web is not that different from trading using the traditional routes. On the Web, you can:

- Display products and services attractively.

- Take orders effectively and process them promptly.

- Dispatch or deliver the product or service.

- Cause customer interaction/feedback (this maintains a bond with existing clients and builds future business).

In this section we're concentrating on the second item above. A Web page order form usually comes into play as soon as a visitor clicks on a "How to Order product" button, or something similar. Consider the following guidelines:

When crafting the precise wording for a "Cancel Order" button, don't forget to relate this to any Sale of Goods laws that may apply in your country, state or area, if necessary.

1   Clearly define the process through which visitors can choose your products or the services you provide.

2   Translate each stage of this process to components in an order form. If you're dealing in products, consider attaching a "Buy this" button (or equivalent) next to each product.

3   Design a form so visitors know what to do every time. Keep instructions clear, brief and simple. Make meanings unambiguous.

A "Cancel Order" option can ensure you waste less time as the vendor, and shows you've invested time and consideration in addressing how to deal with simple mistakes that customers sometimes make, to the benefit of all.

4   Provide a "Cancel Order" option (see the tips) to apply before and after an order has been given, within reason.

5   Ask a few carefully selected testers to try your form to ensure it is easy to use and works properly as you expect.

6   Consider including a link to your order form on every page.

7   Integrate the HTML form with scripting components if necessary. Discuss these aspects with your Internet Service Provider or Web host especially during the early stages of your designs to avoid wasting time later.

Ensuring you get paid

Getting paid is of course crucial whatever methods you use to deliver your product/service – and it can really make your day. Just ask the baby!

If you're involved in a business which is not totally Internet-based, then you probably already have several payment options set up. But what if you want to set up a system to accept payments through your Web pages?

There's a lot of silly hype surrounding e-commerce. If a credit card call back system works profitably for you, then question why you should spend more time and money trying to change it. Even with all the benefits the Internet has to offer, never forget the awesome power of keeping things simple. Just do what works best for you.

There are several ways of getting paid over the Internet; probably the best, quickest and safest is being able to accept payment by credit card using a secure server as examined on previous pages. However, for small-amount purchases, this method is probably not cost effective or practical for most firms.

Providing payment choices: some current options

However, not everyone wants to – or can – pay by credit card online. A huge group of younger or teenage buyers may not yet have access to their own credit card, yet might be prepared to buy if a suitable alternative were available. This group has money to spend so why not just provide a range of payment alternatives?

One approach is to design your page to prompt visitors to enter specific details of their order and their contact information including telephone and email addresses if available. Then provide your customer with some payment choices, such as the two options below:

Option 1
The customer can omit credit card details but include specific contact telephone and fax numbers. Explain that once a customer hits the "Send" button, a representative will contact them shortly to take down credit card details by phone.

Option 2
Ensure that order information/credit card details can be printed out and sent by fax or mailed to the desired payment address.

Doing business: an activity checklist

For online stores in which an inventory plays a key part, selling wares profitably is of course crucial to success. To get a better feel for what's involved in providing goods or services from a Web page design standpoint, let's take a brief look at a typical checklist covering the entire transaction process:

If you're in business and intend to sell products and services from your site to other countries/states find out how you need to charge Sales Tax (or VAT in the UK), if any. Do your homework to avoid any unwelcome surprises.

Don't try to create a product, then sell it. Instead, look for an existing "hungry" market and create your own information product for it:

1. Go to www.overture.com.

2. Look for the "Advertiser Center", then "Tools".

3. Look for the free "Term Suggestion Tool".

4. Type in a word and see how many people searched for it across Overture's network of search engine partners.

5. Find a market that searches thousands of times every month AND which you like.

6. Build your site, market your product and get rich.

1 Research and establish the potential market demand for specific products and services on the Web (search engines).

2 Create the design layout for all Web pages. (Remember: the design of the Home/Index page is particularly important.)

3 Create the entire text and marketing content for each Web page.

4 Prepare the graphics and integrate them with Web page designs. Possibly include multimedia and animation content.

5 Make it easy to carry out business transactions (for example: design dedicated online forms).

6 Set up a reliable, secure way to accept payment for goods or services (ideally use a secure server to process credit card transactions).

7 From the final designs, convert all content to HTML format and test, test, test before going live. Get opinions and feedback.

8 Publish pages to the Web. Do a "Grand Opening". Send carefully tailored press releases to all interested parties, repeatedly.

9 Make it easy for people to find your Home page (search engines, press releases, secondary advertising, etc.).

10 Promote your site like crazy for at least 6 months to get established. Then ease off, but keep promoting.

Launching, promoting and marketing

In this final chapter, we examine the sometimes tricky business of publishing and promoting a website. We also reveal powerful key techniques to promote and monitor your website through search engines, newsgroups and mailing lists.

Covers

Chapter Fifteen

Pre-launch checking and testing

Once your basic Web design is complete, before uploading your pages to your Web space, test your site using (ideally) several different Web browsers: perhaps Internet Explorer, AOL, Netscape and Opera. Creating a website from scratch involves a surprising variety of skills. Consider the following guidelines:

Some types of website almost certainly won't get indexed with current technology. These include: Flash- and frame-based sites, password-protected pages and "dynamic" pages which contain question marks (?) in the Web address (these websites are usually created using ASP, PERL, or Cold Fusion).

1 When your Web pages are almost complete, consider creating a checklist to prevent "howlers" getting through.

2 Then check all the Web pages for just one type of fault in your list at any one time. If you see other types, resist the temptation to be swayed: you'll pick up those faults in a later cycle.

3 Here's an idea of what to check: spelling, grammar, punctuation, layout, any dead external URL links, style consistency, internal links, download times (especially graphics) and animation.

4 Even after carrying out steps 1, 2 and 3 above, mistakes can still occur. Consider asking another person to check your work using these steps as a guide. Repeat the cycle several times.

As the search engines fight for market share, only the stronger and better stand to survive. Google is without doubt now the most important search engine. However, to get listed on Google.com, your site must have at least one other website linking to it (also listed in Google).

Make sure, BEFORE submitting your site to Google, that you have as many links in place as you can.

Uploading your website

When you're ready to upload or publish your website to the Web, you can use FTP (File Transfer Protocol) software, sometimes called an FTP client. FTP software comes in two main forms:

Software demos, free copies and updates are often available on the CD-ROMs that come with popular computer magazines.

- • As part of existing Web design software. Examples include: Adobe GoLive, Microsoft FrontPage, Macromedia Dreamweaver and NetObjects Fusion. Dreamweaver allows you to automatically identify only the changed files and upload those easily using the Synchronize command.

- • As a separate application. CuteFTP and FTP Explorer are two excellent examples. FTP Explorer is currently free for non-commercial use (www.ftpx.com/) and CuteFTP is available as shareware (www.cuteftp.com/).

Timesaver: whatever FTP software you choose, ensure that it allows you to publish updates or changed pages in addition to regular publishing. Consider the following guidelines:

To compel visitors to keep revisiting, add new and fresh content to your site. Consider ways to separate your site from the crowd. Promote your uniqueness and don't be daunted by the (apparently) better offerings of your competitors. You have a USP that they don't, so use it and build on it!

1 Make sure the format you use for your Web page filenames is correct for your Web host. Many Web hosts use UNIX, so INDEX.HTML, Index.htm and index.html may not be the same. Also, check that you're using the correct filename extension; examples include: .html, .htm, and .shtml.

2 When your Web host allocates you Web space, you should also receive 4 pieces of essential information: (1) the exact Web address to which you upload your site – example: ftp.yourcompany.com or even just www.yourcompany.com (2) your username (3) your password (4) the address (base directory) of the folder to which you upload your site; example: "/usr/www/yourcomp/html", "www", "html", or simply "/".

3 If your site uses Web forms, you may need to know the full Web address that points to the CGI-bin for your site.

4 Read your FTP or publishing documentation. Upload your site. Start your Web browser and view your new website.

Introduction to searching the Web

What is a search engine?

A search engine is a continually updated folder made up of hundreds of thousands or millions of Web pages. Search engines use powerful PCs or "spiders" that continuously visit Web pages to record information including all related links they can find and other information for possible inclusion in their databases.

Usually, the more links a website has pointing to it, the higher it ranks in a search engine's database. Search engine examples include AltaVista (www.altavista.com/), Google (www.google.com) and InfoSeek (http://infoseek.go.com/).

What is a directory?

A directory lists websites in logical categories. To get listed, usually you need to submit your website details to the directory and a human operator, rather than a search engine spider, decides whether to list your site. Examples include: Yahoo! (www.yahoo.com) and Open Directory Project (DMOZ – http://dmoz.org).

Using the search engines and directories

The Web can be likened to a vast unordered library in which new books appear continuously, other books disappear and others may seem to "move" around without warning. Search engines and directories help make sense of this apparent chaos.

Although powerful, search engines and directories are usually easy to use: simply enter the words or phrase you want, then click the "Search" or "Send" button. However, to filter out irrelevant data, learn as much as possible about using relevant search engines and directories. Metacrawlers like www.dogpile.com and www.go2net. com query several search engines at once to seek out the information you want.

The trick or knack is to think of precise words that you want to look for, *not* descriptions or concepts relating to what you want. Also, think of alternatives and whether these might have different meanings in other countries. For example, people in the UK who want to search for "Football" should remember that this represents American football in the USA; the answer is to enter "Soccer" as well as, or instead of, "Football".

Downloading files from the Web can take a frustratingly long time sometimes, especially if you're using a slower speed modem. Ideally, get a Broadband connection. But if you're using a 56Kb modem and, during the download, your Internet connection is broken, you may have to download the file again. To save your sanity, choose a product that can resume downloading from where you left off.

Consider GoZilla (currently free) at: www.gozilla.com/ or GetRight at: www.getright.com/.

Your Web submission strategy

So now you're at the stage of completing your Web page design and have uploaded or published your pages to the Web. Well done! One of the quickest and easiest ways of letting others know about your Web page is to register it with the most important search engines and directories (details overleaf). Consider the steps below:

If you don't want to spend time registering your Web page with multiple search engines, companies are available online who will perform this task for you. For example, you could try: http://www.submit-it.com or the free submission service at: http://www.addme.com/ submission.htm.

1 Enter the site submission Web page address for the search engine/directory you want into your Web browser.

2 Optional – choose the option for "registering a new website".

3 Enter your website details. Usually, you can enter the name of your website or page, your Web and email addresses and other basic contact details. If you're prompted to enter keywords and a description, consider these carefully: see Chapter 13 for details.

4 When complete, "Submit" your details to register your Web presence. You'll then probably receive an email message about your request: keep it for your records.

One of the best ways to boost Web traffic to a new website doesn't even involve search engines directly. Here's how: get your Web address listed on an already high-traffic or "busy" website. Some engines will then rank your site higher as a result.

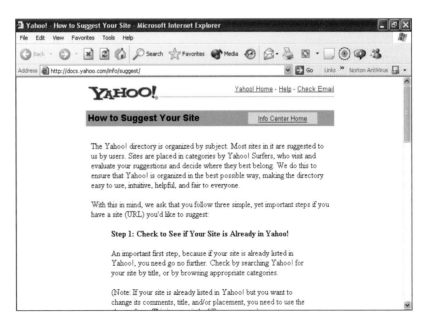

Search engines and Web directories

Consider submitting your website to the most important search engines and Web directories.

Search engines and directories to consider

The current search engine and directory submission Web addresses are often changed without notice as the providers update their services. To find the latest submission page, simply go to the Home/Index page and look for the new link.

Yahoo! is arguably the most important directory for a Web business in which to get listed, while Google is the most important search engine. However, Yahoo! uses people to evaluate whether a site is good enough for the Yahoo! Directory, rather than using Web robot software. Therefore, trying to get listed in Yahoo! may not be easy. As a minimum, everything on your site must work, be up to standard and the site must offer something of particular value to Yahoo! directory users.

- http://www.alexa.com/support/get_archive.html

- http://addurl.altavista.com/addurl/new

- http://search.aol.com/add.adp (results from Google.com)

- http://www.alltheweb.com/add_url.php3

- http://www.google.com/addurl.html

- http://www.hotbot.com

- http://insite.lycos.com/searchservices/

- http://infoseek.go.com/

- http://www-uk.lycos.com/service/addasite.html

- http://submitit.bcentral.com/msnsubmit.htm

- http://www.nationaldirectory.com/addurl/

- http://www.northernlight.com/docs/regurl_help.html

- http://dmoz.org/add.html (also for AOL Netfind)

- http://www.overture.com/ (bid for keywords)

- http://www.scrubtheweb.com/addurl.html

- http://www.search.com/

- http://www.webcrawler.com/info.wbcrwl/

- http://www.whatUseek.com/addurl.shtml

- http://www.yahoo.com/ (results now come from Google.com) http://docs.yahoo.com/info/suggest/ and http://www.yahoo.co.uk/

- http://www.yell.co.uk/

Search engine secrets revealed

Your website is like a tiny island in a huge ocean, so getting noticed is an important aim – and essential for business sites. Getting a high ranking in a search engine even on a single keyword can bring huge numbers of visitors to your website!

1. When considering keywords, note several complementary words/phrases that could point to what you want. Example: if searching for *global warming*, also try *ozone depletion*.

2. Consider resubmitting your website(s) to the search engines about once every 4–6 weeks. Why? Search engines may not automatically update their listings to seek new content.

3. Read individual search engine rules before submitting your site. Ideally, submit your site to each search engine individually rather than using site submission software. Don't resubmit your Web URL too often: some search engines penalize "over submission".

4. Google now supplies search results for AOL Search and Yahoo, so it is now the most important search engine on the Web. Getting listed in Google can get your site listed in other key places too.

5. At Overture.com, you can bid for and purchase keywords that visitors might use to find your website. This approach could be profitable and worthwhile! Discover more at www.overture.com/.

Here's an interesting strategy. Rather than try to get into Yahoo.com, consider submitting through local versions of Yahoo, like yahoo.co.uk/ first instead. Why? Getting listed in a local version may be easier, and once listed, you may have automatic listing in the main directory too.

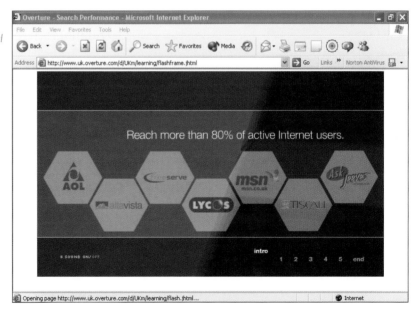

High search engine positioning

Get your Web listed in the first 30 search returns

Imagine: create a highly valuable information product worth at least 5 or 6 times (or more) to the consumer than what you sell it for. Guidelines given in your information product can immediately recover the cost of the product 6 times over. You don't want to be greedy so you sell it on your website for a reasonable $29.

Recently, in a bid to continually improve their services and obviate cheating, the major search engines used a technique called "theme-based indexing" to rank and categorize websites. So, in theory, those websites that concentrate on a particular theme stand to benefit more. However, don't invest all of your efforts into one approach as the ranking method can change quickly.

Assume your website now generates 50,000 hits/month. Only 3% decide to buy; 3% of 50,000 gives us 1500 x $29 = $43,500. Multiply that by 12 (months) = $522,000/year. Imagine your website development + ongoing costs are $5,000. Your product's total annual development + ongoing costs = in the range $10,000–$15,000. So your grand total outlay is $20,000 maximum. Annual profit = $502,000.

The key to this reasonably achievable level of success is the number of targeted hits a website generates, which also translate into sales. *People only visit and revisit a website that offers them a strong reason to visit!* Something free, yet which is valuable, saves them money, helps them earn more money, etc. Key areas include: money, love, health, food, travel and gaining knowledge or skills.

Although this example can make the job look easy, in reality the task involves a considerable amount of work: rework and constant re-promotion are usually required. Also, the search engines and directories continually change their ranking rules. Nevertheless, software like WebPosition Gold can help you keep up-to-date.

When people use search engines, even though their search may return hundreds or even thousands of possible websites, most view only the first 30–50 or so links. Your goal is to get your website listed as high as possible within the first 30 returns for a particular search word or phrase.

If you can achieve this "far from easy" task, your website traffic, or number of visitors or hits, will probably soar to incredible heights! If you apply the techniques outlined in this book successfully, a proportion of visitors will almost certainly buy.

The key: effective and thorough search engine positioning software

WebPosition Gold (WPG) software can help ensure your site is placed high in the search engines. WPG contains 7 key modules: Page Generator, Page Critic, Upload Manager, Submitter, Reporter, Scheduler and Traffic Analyzer. You can download a (currently free) demo from FirstPlace Software at: www. webposition.com/.

Website promotion: top tips

To gain most from your Web pages, you need to actively promote them both on the Web and offline. There are several ways in which you can do this; your choices depend on whether your Web pages are business-oriented or more for personal or hobby use. Consider these guidelines:

Those who are serious about website positioning and gaining higher ranking should check their site's position regularly, and modify their strategy accordingly. Powerful submission software like WebPosition Gold can help make the job much easier.

For businesses, Web cards could be worth considering as part of a promotion project. Web cards are about the size of a postcard and contain a picture of your Home page on one side and other key details. Ideal for special offers etc.

Alternatively, even car number plate stickers could work wonders in high-population centres (but check the legal requirements first).

1 Seek out complementary websites; both parties could benefit from cross-linking. Email the Webmaster and discuss ideas.

2 Create a benefit-packed email signature; consider the guidelines provided on the following pages. Ensure your email software includes this signature on all emails you send.

3 "Register" or broadcast your website correctly with the key search engines and directories as discussed in this chapter.

4 If you're in business, use traditional and non-traditional routes for advertising your new website. Create a compelling press release. Tip: gain an editor's attention using an unusual topic, theme, problem-solving or human interest angle. Then send this to a range of carefully selected promotional sources.

5 Newsgroups and mailing lists can provide another avenue for promotion – if used with consideration. People who share a common interest or have something to say can post articles; start and take part in discussions; seek help to solve a problem; and announce something new. Caution: first read the guidelines provided later in this Chapter.

6 People like quizzes, contests and promotions! By hosting and regularly updating something appropriate like this, you can interact more with your visitors to stimulate and maintain further interest in your Web pages.

Tapping the full power of email

Effective use of the Internet can, without doubt, make business communications easier and cheaper. Sending an email is much cheaper than using the phone: one reason why hundreds of millions are sent around the world each day. Try to integrate email communications closely with your Web page designs and branding to fully benefit.

Some browsers include email built in. However, for more power and flexibility, you can use separate email software. Two popular ones are Eudora: www.qualcomm.com and Pegasus Mail: www.pmail.com/.

A range of excellent free or low-cost email applications are available, including Microsoft's Outlook Express and Outlook, AOL, Netscape Messenger, Pegasus and Eudora.

To ensure the maximum number of recipients can read and see your email message properly, keep to plain text (ASCII) format (not HTML) or Rich Text Format (RTF). If possible, avoid using indents, tabs and justified alignments. Set the word wrap at about 65 characters to reduce eye strain on your readers. Just type your message using simple 4- or 5-line paragraphs. When you enter a Web or email address, your email software may automatically underline it in blue to show it's a hyperlink.

If you have a "true" domain (like "yourcompany.com") you can create a range of professional, effective and easy to remember "departments". For example: orders@yourcompany.com, support@ yourcompany.com, quiz@yourcompany.com, help@ yourcompany.com.

Currently, Microsoft's Outlook Express email and newsreader comes free with Internet Explorer. Outlook Express allows you to set up multiple email signatures and email "identities", so you can use one for private use and one or more for business use.

Creating powerful, compelling email signatures

An email signature is a brief text message (ideally under about 7 lines) that automatically accompanies any email message you send. For businesses, an email signature is a kind of business card. Most email software includes commands to set up email signatures; see your email guide for details.

You could include essential contact information: (optionally, your name, postal address, telephone/fax numbers and email/Web addresses). Your email signature can be formal or friendly and you can create several different email signatures for different purposes.

For businesses, consider also including a slogan or brief but striking benefit-packed phrase describing something important, relevant, or new linked to a Web/email address.

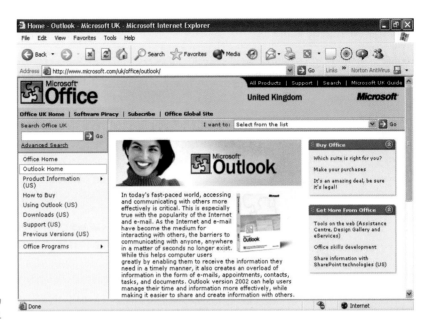

Experiment with email signatures. You can also include special characters top and bottom to "frame" the text content. Just remember that signatures that are seen as too long, too wordy, or just too pushy can do more harm than good. Sometimes, a "soft-sell" approach stands out better.

Example 1: general soft-sell email signature:

Brian Austin MISTC
computer author, trainer, Internet strategist.
e: b.austin@iwesc.com
w: http://www.iwesc.com

Example 2: a more business-oriented signature:

brian@internettips.com
http://www.internettips.com
Access the freedom and perks of the writer's life. Discover how to write and sell what you know on the Web, start a home-based Web business, or create your own Members Only site.

When sending an email to a newsgroup, you can modify it as below to prevent automatic scanners capturing your email address and sending you unwanted mail.

Example: j.smith(NOSPAM)@ jstop20.com (remove NOSPAM before replying).

Example 3: a quick, powerful, benefit-packed signature:

John Smith
http://www.js-top20.com/
Your website in the Top 20, or your money back!
Call toll free now: 800-123-4567

Marketing through the newsgroups

A newsgroup is a computer-based storage area on the Internet containing a collection of articles or messages on a particular topic. Newsgroups and mailing lists are simply the Internet equivalent of clubs. Tens of thousands of different newsgroups and mailing lists exist covering thousands of different topics.

Free Agent is another excellent newsreader. Currently free for non-commercial use: www.forteinc.com/.

People who share a common interest or have something to say can post articles, start discussions, get help and announce something. Anyone can post to a newsgroup or read newsgroup postings. Newsgroups can be accessed through the Internet using a News reader, like the currently free Outlook Express from Microsoft.

Marketing a product or service to a newsgroup

Promoting a product/service is possible through some newsgroups and can be effective, although many won't tolerate commercial advertising. Check what is acceptable first. Solve a problem! Offer free advice! Be genuinely helpful and many newsgroups will tolerate a discreet link to your website in your email signature when you contribute in the newsgroup. Organizations who break the unwritten rules can get banned, spammed or flamed (a barrage of high-volume emails). Sometimes warnings may be sent to the perceived offender before action may be taken.

Avoid blatant and repeated unsolicited advertising of any products or services to ensure that you don't anger other newsgroup members. The one exception is if the newsgroup to which you're promoting explicitly states that they do accept commercial advertising. Check the details.

Newsgroups: top tips

1 If you're considering posting an article, make up a list of all the relevant newsgroups. You can usually download all the newsgroup titles available to you through your dial-up connection from your Internet Service Provider.

2 Avoid using your "real" email address: consider using a format similar to that in the HOT TIP on page 181. Why? See the tip on the left. Or consider getting and using another email address: some generous providers like Microsoft's Hotmail service (www.hotmail.com) can provide free email addresses.

Regularly taking part in newsgroups is one of the fastest ways to get a lot of "spam" email. Some people may "gather" or harvest email addresses from newsgroups without the users' permission, then add the email addresses to a spam mailing list and sell it to other parties for another round of "spamming".

3 Before contributing to a newsgroup, watch how others submit and answer questions and note what level of advertising is "tolerated".

4 If you're still unsure, email the Sysop or newsgroup administrator direct and ask about the rules.

5 Design an appropriate message. Keep it simple, brief and to the point. Make a useful, valuable contribution.

6 Post your message in all the *relevant* newsgroups. However, don't send your message to more than five newsgroups at any one time: if a newsgroup becomes saturated, your message may become lost and recipients may become irritated by the excessive repetition (spamming).

7 If you break the rules by mistake, apologize as soon as possible but never reply to personal email insults or flames.

Using mailing lists

A mailing list and a fax broadcast are essentially different versions that achieve the same result. With an opt-in email mailing list, you can contact tens of thousands of people around the world who have previously given their permission to receive information from you.

You can find mailing lists using the Internet search engines and at mailing list directory sites such as: http:// www.reference.com/.

However, most of these lists are to allow people to share information, skills, solutions and ideas freely. Anyone wanting to sell goods and services on a regular basis shouldn't consider mailing lists as the main avenue of business. Mailing list contributors can react very negatively against those blatantly carrying out "excessive" commercial activities or sending "spam".

Although no laws exist to stop companies advertising in the mailing lists, a lot of grief can be avoided by respecting the right to privacy of individuals against excessive commercialism. Although mailing lists are not really designed with commerce in mind, brief commercial details included at the end of a useful message are usually tolerated, provided these details are discreet.

Also, if the contribution received by the participants in the list is perceived to be especially valuable and worthwhile, news about such contributions can be spread quite quickly, creating profitable alliances without causing offence.

If you're in business, you can use mailing lists to generate useful contacts, sales leads and eventually income. For best results, you can create your own "ezine" mailing list, which can often provide a lucrative income stream over time, as your subscribers get to know and trust you.

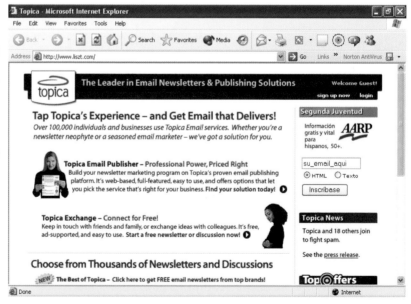

Utilizing your Web statistics

A good Web host provide a range of additional benefits as well as renting Web space. Some can log the number of "hits" to your site and also provide demographic data such as where your visitors are located and so on. Essential for businesses! WebTrends is one particularly powerful tracking software used; if your Web host does not already have this installed, ask if they'll install it for you to use.

In addition to checking your Web statistics, also monitor your website's position submitting it to the search engines. Consider looking at the following tools and resources:

- *http://www.free-webmaster-tools.com/PositionAnalyzer.htm*

- *http://www.marketleap.com/verify/default.htm*

- *http://www.sethi.org/tools/eyespy/*

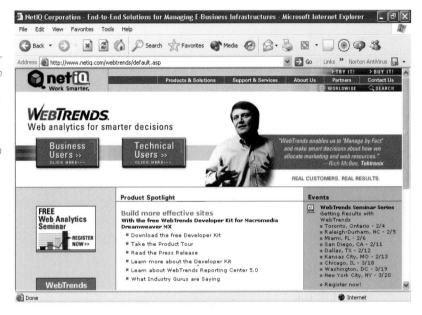

The Site-Reporter Component for NetObjects Fusion users from http:// club.coolmaps.com can calculate essential statistics like upload time and typical browser download times, and check links and images.

Some Web design software can work with plug-ins that monitor your Web designs to help identify problems before you publish a site to the Web.

Using unique reply references

If you're providing some interactive element in your website, like quizzes or prizes, here's another way to test your Web page response. Invite people to reply quoting a unique reference number along with the other information you're requesting. You'll then know respondents could only have seen this particular reference on your Web page.

Using these kinds of approaches, you can build a profile of who your contacts are, where they live, what their interests are and similar information.

Some final thoughts

Maintaining the momentum

To make a website really work, it's not a bad idea to pretend that it's never really finished. In other words, to encourage new visitors and prompt previous visitors to return, plan to actively promote, publicize and update it with new and interesting content regularly.

Consider the following pointers to help you devise new ways to encourage visitors to return:

Why not use this book as your "personal Web success workbook"? Highlight relevant parts, mark pages and scribble your own notes in the margins. With just a little extra work applying the techniques in this book, you could recover your small investment thousands of times over – and why not?

Go for it – and why not invite me to your millionaire party :-)

- Regularly look for ideas to generate schemes which you think would appeal to your visitors.

- Find your visitors' "Hot" buttons i.e. learn what they really want from your website and try to provide it.

- Try to find ways of interacting with previous visitors. For example: if you have previously obtained details of an individual's date of birth, you could email birthday congratulations several days before the event with no strings attached, other than simply mentioning the Web page and inviting your customer to revisit. You could perhaps even include a mention of birthdays on the website. However, consider this carefully; remember, some people may be sensitive about their age being revealed openly.

- Update a static site. Perhaps bring in multimedia, Flash- and ActiveX-type components to help provide the illusion of fresh, new, exciting active content. Also, consider publishing genuine updates through traditional and non-traditional avenues, press releases, plus explore "wacky" ideas, etc.

Recently, I was reading about a restaurant which announced that they had the world's most expensive hamburger: US $41, cheese extra. The story spread across the USA, the UK, Europe and Asia. Every time the "story" was discussed, guess whose name was mentioned: the very people who really only wanted free publicity in the first place. Now you go and do something similar.

A personal Thank You

Thank you for buying and using *Web Page Design in easy steps*. I know there's a lot to think about in this book – that's where the value lies!

You can take your time. Work at your own pace, doing a little every day to achieve your goals. Or you can get serious and set yourself ambitious targets. Most of all, have fun! Don't be afraid to make mistakes – everybody else has at some stage – just learn from them and move on. Now why not go and make your mark – even your fortune – in Cyberspace? Think big and good luck!

Index